PANDEMIC SURVIVAL

It's Why You're Alive

Ann Love & Jane Drake   Illustrated by **Bill Slavin**

TUNDRA BOOKS

Published in Canada by Tundra Books, a division of Random House of Canada Limited,
One Toronto Street, Suite 300, Toronto, Ontario M5C 2V6

Published in the United States by Tundra Books of Northern New York,
P.O. Box 1030, Plattsburgh, New York 12901

Library of Congress Control Number: 2012951554

Library and Archives Canada Cataloguing in Publication

Love, Ann
      Pandemic survival : it's why you're alive / by Ann Love
and Jane Drake ; illustrated by Bill Slavin.

Includes index.
ISBN 978-1-77049-268-4. – ISBN 978-1-77049-499-2 (EPUB)

      1. Epidemics—Juvenile literature. 2. Communicable
diseases—Juvenile literature. I. Love, Ann II. Slavin, Bill
III. Title.

RA653.5.L69 2013   j614.4   C2012-907061-0

We acknowledge the financial support of the Government of Canada through the
Canada Book Fund and that of the Government of Ontario through the Ontario Media
Development Corporation's Ontario Book Initiative. We further acknowledge the support of
the Canada Council for the Arts and the Ontario Arts Council for our publishing program.

ONTARIO ARTS COUNCIL
CONSEIL DES ARTS DE L'ONTARIO

Edited by Sue Tate and Samantha Swenson
Designed by Leah Springate
The artwork in this book was rendered in pen and ink and watercolor.

www.tundrabooks.com

Printed and bound in China

1 2 3 4 5 6   18 17 16 15 14 13

CONTENTS

THE iNDUSTRiAL AGE
(1800–1900): PROSPERiTY, POLLUTiON, and PANDEMiCS

ANTiBiOTiCS
BEFORE and AFTER

GLOBAL ViLLAGE

To our family and friends who make the world a healthier place—doctors, nurses, writers, social workers, biologists, environmentalists, artists, lobbyists, caregivers, coaches, advocates, and more
—A.L. and J.D.

To Geoff, who has always had a fascination with germs
—B.S.

Acknowledgments

Biz Agnew; Henry Barnett; Will Barnett; Alyson Barnett-Cowan; Kim Beatty; Sharon Bentley; Kai Byrom; Brian, Jim, Madeline, and Stephanie Drake; Domenico Inzitari; Donatella Lippi; Adrian, David, Jennifer, and Melanie Love; David and Elizabeth Morley; Helen and Tom Morley; Marie Muir; Oxford Country Public Health and Emergency Services; Roisin Osborne; Evan, Luke, and Olivia Racine; Paul Randall; Mark, Mason, and Sadie Salmoni; Emily Thring; Neil Watters.

Many thanks to the Tundra team—especially Sue Tate, Samantha Swenson, and Sylvia Chan. What a pleasure to work with Bill Slavin again—he puts a whole new spin on "going viral."

Living Proof

An unknown virus that swept through the South Pacific last week, leaving thousands dead, has now spread into China and North America. Today, the Ministry of Health in Beijing reported 248 suspected cases and 17 deaths, while the Center for Disease Control and Prevention in Atlanta, Georgia, reported 13 cases in Seattle.

As a preventative measure, public health officials advise children between the ages of eight and fourteen to bathe in hot goat's urine, whip their backs with knotted ropes until they bleed, or kiss a mouse four times daily. If a child develops stinging, red eyes and a barking cough, parents should immediately apply burning metal pokers to the skin in front of the child's ears or wrap the child in a bundle of wet leaves before laying in an open fire. Authorities recommend all house cats be destroyed.

Does that sound crazy? Maybe …

The average healthy kid today will catch many colds, flus, and other contagious diseases—and get better again—before leaving school. But a hundred years ago, a child's chances weren't so good. In distant times, terrible plagues, epidemics, and pandemics spread around the world and wiped out entire families and even whole communities. At some point, most kids in the past must have sneezed, coughed, felt dizzy, bent over with a cramp, spiked a fever, or woke up with red spots on their skin—and feared for their future. Survivors watched helplessly as beloved parents, sisters, brothers, and friends died in the grips of a scary epidemic.

Depending on where and when they lived, people tried amazing treatments—many based on superstition—to prevent and cure

1

infectious diseases, including all the "recommendations" suggested by the officials in the scenario above. Because of the persistent, even desperate efforts and hopes of ordinary people, we now know which cures work.

Although the treatments often didn't help and many died, the ancestors of kids today—reaching back thousands of years—recovered. Everyone alive now is a descendant of survivors.

This book tells stories from the greatest plagues, poxes, and pestilences in history—and about how people learned to overcome them. Whether the stories happened last year or hundreds of years ago, you are connected to each one in a direct way. Survival is in your blood.

Talk about Sick!

Your throat feels raw when you swallow and your head aches. Even the backs of your eyeballs are sore. Chills run up your back and—oh!— you feel weak at the knees. You're getting sick, but how sick? Are you still well enough to do homework or walk the dog?

It's not likely an allergy, not with a sore throat. You've caught something— the flu, perhaps. You're probably infectious. To avoid passing it on, you better sneeze into your sleeve.

Maybe you're not sick enough to go to the doctor. At this point, she'd probably tell you it's a virus and advise you to drink lots of fluids, take it easy, and come back if you feel much worse.

Once, you remember, it did get worse. You had a raw throat, high fever, and pounding headache. The

doctor took a swab and, a few days later, wrote you a prescription for antibiotics because you tested positive for streptococcus, a bacterium (not a virus). Another time, you had a fever and stomach troubles and she did tests looking for some gross parasite like an amoeba or protozoan. Fortunately, that turned out to be negative.

Viruses, bacteria, and parasites that prey on humans are microscopic predators called pathogenic microbes. They cause infectious diseases and spread from one person to another mostly through touch, the air we breathe, and the water we drink. Some microbes spread from the environment to people through animals, especially insects.

When an infectious disease spreads from person to person, it's called communicable. A contagious disease spreads rapidly. If a severe infectious disease spreads rapidly and widely, it's an epidemic. When an epidemic jumps from country to country, even across oceans to other continents, it's called a pandemic.

Not all microbes cause serious illness (are pathogenic), and not all diseases make you so sick that you need medical attention. Your body is an amazing self-healing machine and can fight off many infections on its own by not allowing them to spread or worsen. Between birth and early adulthood, an average kid gets sick more than two hundred times with different microbial infections, building up immunities in order to fight off contagious diseases that may cycle back again. If you get measles once, for example, you likely won't get it again.

When you get sick—even with just a

mild cold—you notice your symptoms and often share the gory details with your friends. It's natural. Your ancestors did this, too. This tendency to observe and keep track of the progress of an illness helps humans survive.

Our ancient ancestors tried every imaginable way to avoid getting sick. Over time, they learned what worked and why. They discovered that bathing in goat's urine doesn't prevent illness but that washing hands in soapy water can—especially before meals, after bathroom visits, and after contact with someone who is sick.

We now know that it's easier to stay healthy if we shower or bathe regularly, eat nutritious food that has been carefully handled and prepared, drink clean water, and live in pest-free spaces. In order to protect ourselves and our friends from germs, we dispose of used tissues, we don't spit in public, we keep our vaccinations up-to-date, and we sneeze into our sleeves.

This book uses medical terms—virus, bacterium, parasite, microbe, pathogen, infection, contagion, vaccination, antibiotic, pandemic, immunity, and more. If you get bogged down with these buzz words, check the glossary at the back of the book. Being able to name the problem can help solve it. Use the index to find recurrences of epidemics and the conditions that helped their spread. Making sense of sickness is something you can pass on—to help yourself and others stay healthy.

Bacterial Invasion

When you get home from school, do you head straight to the kitchen and plunk down your backpack to make a snack? If you take a look around, you don't have to look past the surface. Everything in sight—counters, doorknobs, appliances, even this book—is smeared with millions and millions of microscopic bacteria cells.

Do you remember wiping up slopped milk this morning and then tossing the cloth in the sink? That damp heap is a germ's delight—a passive host for rapid bacterial growth. And the unwashed cutting board you used to make a cheese sandwich? It's currently teeming with tens of millions of bacterial organisms you'll never see. Should we talk about the bathroom? Didn't think so.

Before you were born, while you developed in your mother's womb, you bathed in amniotic fluid—a sterile, bacteria-free liquid. This environment

helped you, as a fetus, to grow in a healthy way.

From the moment you were released into the world, bacteria have bombarded you, entering through your mouth, nose, scratches, and insect bites. Bacteria live in, on, and around your body. And your hands host more bacteria than any other part of your body. Most of the time, you are totally unaware of the presence of bacteria. In fact, at any given moment, you are carting around ten times more bacteria cells than human cells.

Generally, there are three kinds of bacteria: the good, the neutral, and the bad. One of your body's first orders of

business was to populate your intestines with good, friendly bacteria called flora. You can't live without flora. Many microscopic bacteria have a symbiotic relationship with your body—you supply them with nourishment and they do the body's work.

Good bacteria are essential for digestion, converting food to usable nutrients such as vitamins, protecting you from harmful bacteria, and much more. It's perfectly normal to have at least five hundred different kinds of good bacteria in your intestines at any given time. Some bacteria, good and neutral, are just passing through. They enter through the usual openings and exit in your feces, aka poop. They don't bother you, and your immune system ignores them. That's not the case with bad bacteria.

One classic bad bacterium is *Salmonella typhimurium*—salmonella, for short. If you've suffered from this, it's unlikely you'll ever forget it. The first sign that this bacterium is churning in your system is nausea and feeling revolted by the idea of eating. Then, deep in the bowels, cramping starts, and you take up residence on the toilet, where you produce watery diarrhea and experience severe stomach pain. These symptoms can last for as long as a week. What poisoned you?

You won't like the answer.

People become infected with salmonella after eating food—usually chicken or eggs—that has been contaminated by animal feces containing salmonella. In the case of eggs, salmonella can be present on improperly washed eggshells or already inside the egg's yolk, passed from the

Bacteria Fact-eria

In 1676, Dutch scientist Antony van Leeuwenhoek magnified a specimen of human body fluid using his primitive microscope and saw "animalcules." Leap forward to 1828, Christian Gottfried Ehrenberg, a German scientist studying microscopic organisms, coined the terms bacterium (singular) and bacteria (plural). With bacteria now in view, scientists had a lot to learn.

Most bacteria are single-celled organisms that can live on their own. As long as they have a food source, they are free to live, eat, and reproduce. Bacteria reproduce by binary fission, which means that an individual bacterium will double in size and then divide into two, resulting in identical twin cells. Then those two cells each divide again to produce another pair of identical twin cells. So one becomes two, two becomes four, four becomes eight, and so on.

This reproduction happens fast—at an average rate of twenty minutes a generation. After twenty-four hours, one bacterium can transform into a family of ten million identical bacteria.

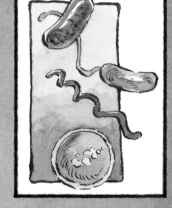

Bacteria usually look like commas, spiral noodles, microscopic hairy hotdogs, strands of pearls, or clusters of tiny beads. Many bacteria are classified by shape, and the scientific terms we use to identify them are bacillus (rod-shaped, from the Latin word for "stick"), vibrio (curved and comma- shaped), spirillum (helical or tightly coiled), and coccus (spherical, from the Greek word for "seed").

hen to the egg while the egg was still inside her body. Sometimes salmonella spreads in a food-processing plant after a hygienic breakdown. Cooking the food to a temperature of 165°F (74°C) will kill the bacteria.

In September and October of 1994, the Minnesota Department of Health reported a sudden spike in the number of people sick with salmonella. After several weeks of detective work, government officials determined that the culprit was a locally produced ice cream. The same tank truck had been used to ship liquid eggs to one factory and then used later to transport a pasteurized ingredient called premix to the ice cream factory. The truck had been cleaned between shipments, but a valve had not been properly sanitized.

A total of 740 confirmed cases of salmonella were reported across thirty states, with another 3,423 more unconfirmed cases over forty-one states. After a huge recall of ice cream, the company changed their trucking policy. Eggs and premix no longer mix!

Viral Attack

Katie felt bone-weary as she packed her sleepover bag. Her eyes watered and she had a nagging, ticklish scratch at the back of her throat. A stupid little sniffle wouldn't keep her from her best friend's birthday party!

She felt OK through the pizza and games, but by present-opening time, her head was aching and the sinuses in her cheeks throbbed. Still, she kept her symptoms to herself. A dozen twelve-year-olds laid out their sleeping bags in clock formation on the carpeted floor, their heads together in the middle. They gossiped late into the night, with Katie stifling coughs and her voice becoming a hoarse whisper before she finally fell asleep mid-sentence.

The next morning, when her mom came to pick her up, Katie had a full-blown, rotten cold. Over the next few days, nine of her eleven friends also got sick, as did many of their siblings, some of their parents, grandparents, teachers, classmates, teammates, and coaches. Katie unwittingly infected several hundred people with the virus known as the common cold—and, in doing so, she increased sales in tissues, ginger ale, chicken soup, cold medication, and vitamin C.

Viruses are primitive microbes that, on their own, are not alive—but they are not exactly dead, either. They are very simple structures that are activated only when they attach themselves to a living cell, or "host." And viruses are attracted to specific hosts that provide a favorable environment for them.

Like Katie at the party, the virus rings your immune system's doorbell. If your immune system is weakened, you're open for visitors and viruses force their way into the cells in your body. In the case of the common cold, the virus targets cells in the mucous of the nose and throat. Then individual viral particles take over host cells and start reproducing inside the cells. Eventually, the host cells explode, spewing out viral particles that look for new, receptive host cells. Not all

viruses act the same, but the results of infection are the same: the mass production of virus cells and the death of host cells.

When your body senses a viral infection, it sounds an alarm—like a home security system—signaling to the immune system to launch a counterattack. Fever, cough, and phlegm are the body's weapons. Fever raises your core temperature, killing off viruses. And sneezing, coughing, and hacking up spit force some of the virus particles out of the mouth and nose.

In the late 1800s, rival scientists were aware that viruses existed but lacked the equipment to prove it.

Frenchman Louis Pasteur was one of the scientists. In 1885, he thought rabies was caused by a germ too small to be seen under the microscope. Pasteur referred to the tiny microbe as a virus, derived from the Latin word for "poison." He is credited with being the pioneer of virology.

Seven years later, Dmitri Ivanovski, a Russian biologist, isolated the microbe that was attacking tobacco plants. He created a syrup from crushed leaves from infected plants and passed the syrup through a porcelain (pottery) filter. With this, he demonstrated that a microbe smaller than bacteria actually passed through the filter. Then he wiped the leaves of healthy plants with the syrup. When they became infected he proved there was something there—viruses. A few years later, Germans Friedrich Loeffler and Paul Frosch also used filters to isolate the tiny infectious organism causing foot-and-mouth disease. A virus? Yes!

Viruses finally came into view after the 1931 invention of the electron microscope. Powered by the ability to magnify specimens a million times more than an ordinary light microscope, scientists could not only see that viruses existed, they could also begin to figure out their structure, function, and behavior.

Viral Fact-eria

A viral cell is tiny and consists of a protein shell wrapped around genetic matter. When a virus invades another organism, it uses the larger cell's complex structure to reproduce itself. Viruses can remain dormant and then reactivate themselves. The chicken pox virus stays in the body after a full recovery. One-third of kids who get the chicken pox virus will develop another form of the virus—shingles—as an adult. HIV is another example of a virus that does not necessarily start reproducing as soon as it finds a host.

As early as 200 BC, people protected themselves from infectious diseases using a form of inoculation. Vaccines remain an effective way to prevent many viruses from taking hold. By exposing the immune system to a controlled amount of a virus or a copy of part of the virus, the body learns to recognize that virus and will fight it off if the real virus turns up in the future. Some drugs, such as Tylenol, help control symptoms; and antiviral drugs slow or prevent the onset of certain viral illnesses. Antibiotics have no effect on viruses.

Prions

Squish the words *protein* and *infection* together and you get *prion*. A little different from viruses but also activated within living cells, prions are microscopic, non-living protein particles responsible for a rare brain-wasting disease in humans called Creutzfeldt-Jakob disease. Some hoofed animals including cows, sheep, moose, and deer can get brain-wasting prion diseases. Cats, ostrich, and mink can also be affected. Prion diseases are rapidly progressing and are always fatal. There is no cure.

Bugs and the Bloodstream

At night, by the edge of a tropical forest, a female mosquito looks for a blood meal. Without fresh blood, her eggs will not mature. She is attracted to the warmth, smell, and breath of a sleeping human family. The carbon dioxide–rich air exhaled by the father grabs her attention—and his bare shoulder is not protected by the mosquito netting. She lands on his warm skin, numbs it with a drop of her saliva—which also slows the time it will take for his blood to clot—and drinks her fill. The mosquito flies away to rest and digest.

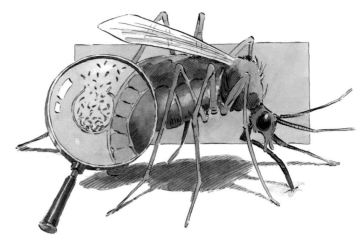

Several days later, she lays her first batch of eggs in a puddle and moves on to find another blood meal to feed a second batch. She will lay as many eggs as she possibly can in the few weeks of her short life.

What the female mosquito doesn't know is that her victim, the father, is a malaria carrier. His blood contains a tiny parasitic creature, a protozoan, of the species Plasmodium. *The father is lucky—he survived childhood malaria. But he still suffers regular bouts of fever, chills, and weakness.*

His infected blood sits in the female mosquito's gut and, because she is a kind of Anopheles *mosquito, her body can't easily fight the parasite. (Of more than three thousand species of mosquitoes in the world, about 450 are* Anopheles *mosquitoes. But fewer than forty species of* Anopheles *mosquitoes will carry malaria.)*

The Plasmodium *in the mosquito's gut transforms into thousands of minute wriggling banana-shaped forms, which then invade her salivary gland. The mosquito will infect the next human she bites.*

A week later, two brothers who live near the tropical forest stay out playing soccer until dark. On their way home, the infected female mosquito senses their heat. She rises from the damp grass beside the path and bites the younger brother on his ankle. She drinks her fill of his blood—while injecting about two dozen of the Plasmodium *parasites into his bloodstream. The mosquito flies away before the boy senses her bite and swats his leg.*

The boy continues to walk home, feeling nothing except the bothersome itch of the mosquito bite. But the Plasmodium parasites travel through his bloodstream to his liver in less than an hour. They wriggle into his liver cells, where they transform again—this time dividing into tens of thousands of triangular-shaped forms of the

protozoan. This process takes a varied amount of time, depending on the kind of Plasmodium.

In about two weeks, the parasites burst out of the liver cells into the bloodstream, where the boy's immune system tries to fight them off. Despite his body's efforts, some manage to penetrate his red blood cells. Inside these cells, most of the parasites change again, consuming and killing the red blood cell hosts. A few remain inactive,

Protozoan Fact-eria

Along with bacteria and viruses, protozoans are a major cause of epidemic disease in humans. Malaria, amoebic dysentery, human African trypanosomiasis (sleeping sickness), and giardia (beaver fever) are all different kinds of protozoan infection. Although bacteria and viruses spread by floating through the air or in fluids, protozoans self-propel to reach new hosts. For example, *Plasmodium*, the malaria-causing protozoan, moves through blood by whipping flagella, or hair-like filaments, outward in all directions.

The malaria-carrying *Plasmodium* protozoan transforms through seven different forms in its life cycle. It also must pass through both a warm-blooded animal (such as a human) and a mosquito to complete the cycle of disease.

For hundreds of years, people connected malaria with swamps—*mal aria* translates from Italian as "bad air"—but not with

mosquitoes. It took the keen observations of a number of doctors to piece the whole malaria puzzle together.

In 1880, Dr. Charles Laveran, a French physician working in a military hospital in Algeria, looked through a microscope at the fresh blood of a soldier who had just died of malaria. He noticed filaments waving like arms inside the red blood cells. He realized that the soldier's blood was infected by a living, moving protozoan. A few years later, Dr. Ronald Ross, a poet and English medical doctor stationed in India, observed that malaria occurred most often in areas infested with mosquitoes. Ross searched for Laveran's malaria parasite in mosquitoes and finally found the protozoan growing in the guts of *Anopheles* mosquitoes. He was able to prove that people bitten by an infected *Anopheles* mosquito develop malaria. He won the Nobel Prize in 1902 for this discovery.

waiting to be sucked up by another Anopheles *mosquito as it feeds.*

When the feeding parasites have destroyed their host red blood cells, they explode out of the spent cells and hunt for fresh ones to attack. They burst out all at the same time so that their combined toxic wastes flood into the boy's bloodstream. His body tries to fight the poison by spiking a fever that causes uncontrollable shivering and shaking. The surviving parasites go on to find healthy red blood cells to invade—and the cycle of consuming and killing red blood cells repeats.

When the parasites enter fresh red blood cells, the boy feels a little better. But every three days, when the parasites burst out of the destroyed red bloods cells and release more toxic waste, he suffers repeated bouts of intense shivering and fever. If the boy loses too many red blood cells, he will become severely anemic and die.

But this boy is lucky. The Plasmodium *he carries in his blood does not kill him. He will suffer terrible periods of fever and chills for years— and will miss many soccer matches— but the intensity of his attacks will lessen. If he is bitten by one of those forty species of* Anopheles *mosquitoes, his parasites will infect that mosquito and then anyone else it bites. Today, in*

Africa, one in every three children dies of malaria—and someone in the world dies of malaria every ten seconds. It's hard to believe the power of a one-celled protozoan.

A doctor probably could cure the boy's malaria with drugs—if his family could afford them. Good mosquito netting can protect those not infected. Meanwhile, scientists scramble to find a vaccine to stop the spread of this protozoan that has stalked humans for thousands of years.

Lifestyle Choices and Chances

Do you want to get sick? Can you find a friend with a cold who'll sneeze their virus on you? If you would prefer a bacterial infection, one that will rip through your gastrointestinal tract, why not leave your sandwich in your locker for a week and then eat it? Even better, find a pond with a beaver dam, drink the water, and get beaver fever— then you can play host to the single-cell protozoan parasite and endure fascinating/disgusting symptoms such as liquid farts, diarrhea, and vomiting.

Really? That sounds ridiculous! Like most people, you try to avoid getting sick whenever possible. And if you do get sick, you want to find

and blame the culprit who made you feel so lousy. Still, there are some non-contagious diseases affecting large numbers of people that are caused by risky lifestyle choices such as drinking alcohol and experimenting with drugs. Smoking, suntanning, and extreme dieting can cause diseases of pandemic proportion later in life.

Smoking

Pull the gold tab on the shiny clear plastic wrapping and you're one step closer. Don't look at the package—it could shock you with graphic photos of rotting gums, scary messages about strokes, or dire deadly statistics. Get the cigarette in your mouth fast, before you change your mind. Grip it with your lips while you strike the match. Now hold the flame to the tip and inhale through the filter. Draw that smoke right down to the bottom of your lungs. After you cough, puke, or sit down from dizziness, think about it. You could become an addict.

The body does not need anything a cigarette has to offer. Each one contains poisonous chemicals, including carbon monoxide. That's the same deadly gas emitted from burning fossil fuels. People install monitors in their homes to alert them of the presence of carbon monoxide!

And then there's formaldehyde, the stuff used to preserve dead frogs in the biology lab, and the tar—doesn't that belong on highways? Despite this toxic brew, three thousand American kids light up for the first time every single day. If they keep smoking, they'll die an average of seven years earlier than non-smokers.

So why do teens smoke?

Tobacco companies use advertising to target the teen market. Adult smokers quit or die, so tobacco companies recruit new young smokers to buy their products. Cigarettes are strategically placed in movies and music videos, and kids watch as their favorite stars make smoking look cool. Teens feel pressure from their peers, and some follow the example of their smoking parents.

Whatever the reason to start, quitting is the hard part. That's because smoking is addictive, and the body craves nicotine as early as after the first cigarette.

Diseases related to smoking kill more Americans than car accidents, suicide, AIDS, homicide, alcohol, and hard drugs—combined. It's the number one preventable cause of death, and secondhand smoke also kills people who don't smoke.

Eating Disorders

One in four American children between the ages of nine and twelve is considered overweight or obese. Kids in all developed countries—ones with advanced economies, such as Canada, Japan, Germany, France, the United Kingdom, Italy, Australia—weigh in similarly. This number is much higher than when your grandparents were young.

Although some people are overweight or obese because of their genetic makeup, most are this way because of lifestyle choices. The excessive eating of unhealthy, often fatty foods combined with increasing inactivity has encouraged weigh gain. Many kids today spend more time in front of the TV or computer or playing video games than playing outdoors—and driving to school and friends' houses rather than walking or cycling isn't helping. Kids aren't totally to blame for this trend. Their parents often have the same habits and don't always see the impact their choices have on their kids.

What's the big deal about obesity? Obesity is directly related to an increased risk of heart disease, diabetes, depression, joint problems, and even cancer. Most people used to believe that obese children would turn into obese adults and then get these illnesses. Now doctors are seeing adult diseases in children as young as nine.

Anorexia nervosa and bulimia are two other food-related illnesses affecting older kids, mostly girls ages twelve and up. Patients deny or purge themselves of food in an effort to control their weight and body image. The causes are complex and hard to pinpoint, but a society that idolizes thinness is, in part, to blame.

Eleven out of every one hundred high school and college students in America have an eating disorder. One in two hundred has anorexia, and four out of every six hundred have bulimia. If a teen has anorexia, he or she is twelve times more likely to die from it than from any other possible cause. Those who survive are more likely to die young due to heart problems or by suicide.

Suntan Versus Skin Cancer

Question: Is there a connection between exposure to direct sunlight and skin cancer?

Answer: Yes. I mean, no! Well, maybe. Err—sometimes?

"Sometimes" is in fact the correct answer. Not everyone who skips sunscreen and uses tanning beds gets skin cancer. And some who always use sunscreen and never use a tanning bed will get malignant melanoma because they were born with a rare genetic tendency to the disease. Still, confusion and denial swirl around this usually preventable problem. Most parents are strict about applying sunscreen to their kids and making them wear hats and protective clothing when venturing out into the sunshine. But girls fifteen and over are increasingly using tanning beds (which have the same effect as direct sunshine) and skipping the sunscreen. Boys and young men are less likely to pay for a suntan but are more likely than girls and women to skip the sunscreen.

One in seven people will develop skin cancer in their lifetime. That's not something teens think about when they go to the beach, ride their bikes, or even ski. The effects of overexposure to sunlight add up over time, presenting as skin cancer later in life. It is well established that ultraviolet radiation (UVR) from the sun and tanning machines causes cancer, and UVR is on the U.S. government's list of elements or substances that cause cancer in people.

Why Soap and Water?

Long ago, when disease was still a mystery, a family of hunters approached a fire pit. Months before, they had used the campsite to roast a tasty loin of wild bison. This time, they

brought with them butchered goat to cook for a feast.

One young woman poked the cold ash in the bottom of the pit with a stick and felt something soft. She bent forward and scraped away the ash with her fingers to clean the pit for their fire. When she finished, a slimy paste covered her hands and gummed under her fingernails. She dipped her hands in a nearby creek and rubbed hard to rinse off the paste. The paste bubbled into a lather and the water washed away all the ashes, dirt, blood, and grease from the hunt. She studied her spotless hands and decided that if she ever found that paste again, she'd roll it into a ball and save it for the next time her hands were filthy.

We're not exactly sure when or where humans first stumbled upon the magical effect of soap and water, but all it would have taken was noticing that rainwater, ash, and fat mixed together form a substance that cleans away grease and dirt. In scientific terms, we might say that a strong alkaline solution such as lye reacts chemically with animal fats or vegetable oils to form crude soap.

Before soap, ancient peoples probably cleaned themselves by scrubbing their skin with sand and then scraping the sand and dirt off with water. But this wouldn't kill or wash away the disease-causing microbes that attach to the oils on our skin.

Today, in the twenty-first century, scientists believe that hand-washing with soap is one of the easiest and most effective ways to avoid catching and spreading disease.

Contagious diseases often travel from person to person through touch. When you are sick, microbes from inside your body transfer to your hands when you blow your nose, put your fingers in your mouth, scratch a rash, or wipe your bottom. If you don't wash your hands right away, you pass those microbes to others and to your surroundings. That's why doctors tell us to sneeze into our sleeves and to always wash our hands after going to the bathroom and before meals.

Your hands can also pick up microbes from the environment and other people when you touch a doorknob, handle money, change a diaper, pet an animal, touch raw meat, and so on. These microbes enter your body when your unwashed hands rub your eyes or nose, scratch your skin, or touch your lips.

Public health specialists say that at least half of all colds and flu are spread by hand-to-hand contact. Hand-washing with soap doesn't totally eliminate the spread of infections—but it's a big help.

How does washing with soap work? Soap loosens the oils on our skin—releasing any cling-on viruses, bacteria, or other pathogens in the process—and water washes them away. But you must lather and rinse your hands front and back, between your fingers, under your nails, and around your wrists for the soap to do its job. And you must wash your hands for at least twenty seconds—that's as long as it takes to sing "Happy Birthday" two times or to recite the alphabet once.

Soaps don't have to be labelled "antibacterial" to be effective—all soaps get rid of bacteria. Some people now choose hand sanitizers over regular soap and water. Hand sanitizers use alcohol to kill microbes, but only work if they contain at least 60 percent alcohol and if you rub your hands until they are completely dry.

ANCIENT STORIES, MODERN DIAGNOSES

Wrath of the Gods

Ten thousand years ago, kids didn't catch many contagious diseases. Epidemics may not have existed. Families lived in small, isolated hunting groups—so disease-causing bacteria and viruses would do the rounds once or twice, run out of victims, and disappear. Most kids died as a result of infected wounds, animal bites, or starvation.

Five thousand years later, that all changed. Farmers learned to grow enough food to support life in towns and cities. Agriculture provided many benefits—in a word, civilization—but the new communities had at least one big drawback: people lived close enough to each other for microbes to spread. And the new cities attracted a steady stream of immigrants from the countryside, refreshing the supply of possible victims.

Around the same time in Asia, the Middle East, and North Africa, people learned to domesticate animals. They kept their precious livestock near or right inside their homes. Many animal diseases mutated into human contagious diseases. Tuberculosis and probably smallpox came from cows, influenzas from pigs and ducks, the common cold from horses, measles from cows or dogs, whooping cough from pigs or dogs, and so on. Disease also passed from animals to humans through the bites of bugs that lived on livestock or in stored food.

Epidemics took hold in the ancient Old World. In North and South America, however, people grew crops and moved into cities and towns but they domesticated just a few animals, such as dogs. As a result, ancient New World peoples didn't catch as many contagious diseases—until the Europeans brought them to North and South American shores.

Early city dwellers didn't think of disease as we do now. A sickness was a sickness and people didn't distinguish between one illness and another. The gods made you sick—they were punishing you or your community for a wrongdoing you may or may not recognize. When large numbers of people fell ill and died, whole communities became frightened—why were the gods so angry? Curing disease required praying and sacrificing for—or appeasing—the right gods. Only gradually did people start to observe differences between illnesses and look for earthly causes and cures.

Hippocrates of Cos, an ancient Greek physician born in 460 BC, was first to record the differences between diseases. He went on to suggest that diseases were caused by imbalances in the body and recommended that physicians treat the patient rather than look to the gods.

Hundreds of years after Hippocrates lived, however, many still believed that angry gods caused disease. And even when doctors schooled by Hippocrates's methods recorded symptoms of patients, they often missed details that we would consider important today. For this reason, it's sometimes hard to identify the diseases the doctors were describing. Only when people started to observe carefully and ask questions about disease did they begin to find answers, cures, and comfort.

Pandora

An ancient Greek story blames the gods for inventing disease.

Long ago, Zeus, the god of sky and thunder, ordered a minor god named Prometheus to create men to live on Earth. Prometheus carefully created these beings. Once finished, he worried his men would lead miserable lives. He asked Zeus if he could give them fire to keep warm at night and predators at bay. But Zeus said fire was sacred—only for the gods. Prometheus, however, disobeyed and gave fire to mortal men.

Zeus was enraged and chained Prometheus to a mountainside rock for eternity. Every day, Zeus sent an eagle to eat Prometheus's liver, and every night the liver grew back to be eaten again the next day.

For men, Zeus ordered a punishment, too. He asked the god Hephaestus to create a beautiful human woman, carved out of white marble. He named her Pandora, "the all-gifted."

Then Zeus ordered other gods and goddesses to endow Pandora with gifts to add to her appeal. The goddesses gave Pandora an alluring smile, ruby red lips, and sapphire blue eyes, and they clothed her in lovely gowns and jewelry. Zeus gave Pandora two gifts: an insatiable curiosity and a sealed jar that she must never open.

Of course, Pandora could not contain her curiosity and opened the jar. Out flew all the evils that humans now endure, including disease. When Pandora realized what she was unleashing, she slapped the lid back on but managed to save only hope inside the jar.

Ever since, humans have suffered from many diseases and evil wrong-doing, but they always have hope.

First Epidemics—Or Not

What were the first epidemics? Where and when did they occur? Historians can't be sure, but they are sniffing out a few leads.

In 2000 BC, more people called Egypt home than any other place on Earth—about two million. Most ancient Egyptians lived in close quarters with both their families and their livestock. These conditions probably ignited the first epidemics. And when Egyptian traders traveled to nearby nations, the epidemic diseases hitchhiked along with them, spreading across the Middle East. Historians think the first epidemics must have been severe because people had no natural defences against them, no idea how to help the sick, and no clue how to avoid catching any contagious disease.

Old stories from the Middle East tell of angry gods inflicting plagues on people and their livestock. These astonishing stories lack the details needed for a diagnosis today, but they could be early attempts to record and explain the first frightening epidemics.

The Plague of Boils

The biblical story of Moses describes ten plagues sent by the Hebrew god YHWH (pronounced Yah-weh) to devastate Egypt. Some historians believe the plagues are based on real events that occurred around 1500 BC.

The book of Exodus tells us that Moses was born of Hebrew parents in Egypt, where the Hebrews were slaves. As a young man, Moses stopped an Egyptian from beating a fellow Hebrew. In the fight that followed, Moses killed the Egyptian and then escaped the country to avoid death himself. After Moses worked forty years as a shepherd in exile, YHWH appeared to him and commanded he return to Egypt and lead his people out of slavery.

Moses traveled to Egypt and demanded that the pharaoh, the Egyptian leader, allow all Hebrews to move to a new land where they could worship their god in their own way. The pharaoh refused, declaring he had never heard of their god.

To punish the pharaoh as well as show his power, YHWH unleashed ten plagues on Egypt—one after the other. The plagues included turning the Nile River to blood, overrunning the land with frogs, unleashing locusts on the crops, and lashing the land with hail—not disease-based plagues, but scary pestilences nonetheless.

The sixth plague—a plague of boils—could have been a disease. The Hebrew god told Moses and his brother to each take handfuls of soot from a kiln and toss the soot into the air in the presence of the pharaoh. The soot spread over the land as a fine dust and caused painful boils to erupt on the skin of the people and on their livestock.

Historians have considered different ancient epidemic diseases that might have caused these skin boils or ruptures. They have narrowed down the possibilities to anthrax, bubonic plague, and smallpox.

Anthrax is a disease that infects cattle, sheep, and humans. People catch it by touching an infected live or dead animal, by breathing in spores of the bacterium, or by eating infected meat. When spread by touch, a person develops an itchy bump at each point of contact, which later erupts into a painful boil. The infection then spreads throughout the body and sometimes causes death. When people breathe in the spores as well, death is common. Anthrax can be a killer when people live with their livestock.

Bubonic plague is a disease passed on to people by the bites of infected fleas that live on rodents, usually rats. Symptoms include buboes, distinctive lumps like boils that appear in the groin and armpits. A written record from 1534 BC in Egypt describes a disease with lumps that sound like buboes. Fossilized fleas carrying bubonic plague bacteria have been found in Amarna, an Egyptian workers' village, dating about 1350 BC.

Smallpox is a disease that developed in humans but probably originated from cattle. In humans, fevers spike and large red pustules not unlike boils erupt on the skin before the sufferers develop complications that can lead to death. Archaeologists have found smallpox scars on three mummies from ancient Egypt. At least one pharaoh, Ramses V, likely died from smallpox—around 1145 BC.

The pharaoh of Moses's time wouldn't set the Hebrews free even after the plague of boils. Before unleashing the final plague, YHWH instructed all Hebrews to mark their doorposts with lamb's blood. At midnight, the Hebrew god sent death to every first-born son in Egypt—except those within marked homes. Even the first-born male young of livestock died.

This plague so shocked the pharaoh that he commanded Moses to lead his people out of Egypt that night, taking whatever they needed. Every spring since then, Hebrews have celebrated Passover, the time when death passed over their ancestors' homes and Moses led them to freedom.

The Hittite Plague

About 1320 BC, the Hittites crowned Mursili II their king. The Hittites rose to power in what is now Turkey. Aside from Egypt, they were the most powerful empire in the Middle East. The Hittites were skilled fighters, feared for their lightning attacks on horse-drawn chariots.

Mursili's father, King Suppiluliuma, killed his older brother, the rightful heir to the throne. Suppiluliuma then waged many wars and conquered many peoples, enlarging the kingdom to the south and east. In the process, he broke an important treaty with Egypt. Egyptian prisoners from those wars brought a disease into Hittite lands, where it spread north and raged for twenty years. Suppiluliuma and one of his sons both died from this plague.

Mursili believed that when Suppiluliuma killed the rightful heir and broke the treaty, he committed sins that angered the gods. Found in the ruins of the Hittite capital city, Mursili's prayer pleads: "And because I have confessed my father's sin, let the soul of the Hattian storm-god, my lord … be again pacified! Take pity on me and drive the plague out of Hatti land!"

What was this plague? Letters from Egyptian spies describe the disease as fast-moving and causing fever, disabilities, and death in humans and animals. Because of this plague, donkey caravans were banned. We have no more information than that—clearly too little for a diagnosis, but top guesses include anthrax, bubonic plague, and smallpox—killers known at the same time in nearby Egypt. Another possibility is rabbit fever, a disease passed on to humans from the bite of a tick that has already bitten an infected rabbit, sheep, or donkey.

Near the end of the Hittite plague, another tribe tried to conquer the weakened Hittites, but they were overcome by plague themselves. Some historians wonder if the Hittites realized that livestock passed on this disease and deliberately set infected sheep outside enemy towns in an early form of bioterrorism.

The Plague of Athens

In 1999, experts in epidemics met at the University of Maryland and put their heads together to determine the cause of the Plague of Athens, which occurred between 430 and 426 BC. The doctors analyzed the list of symptoms recorded by an ancient Greek historian Thucydides, who had caught the disease himself, survived, and wrote down what it felt like. A clear thinker and observer, Thucydides is known as the first modern historian. Despite his good 2429-year-old data, the Maryland meeting may not have found the right answer.

The Plague of Athens broke out during the Peloponnesian War between Athens and Sparta in ancient Greece. People of the time thought Athens had an unbeatable navy, Sparta an invincible land force.

Athens was one of the first known democracies, while Sparta was a kingdom built around military honor. The Athenians extended freedom and voting rights exclusively to their male citizens—and no one else in the world counted. That didn't sit well with other Greeks. Many city states joined Sparta to challenge Athenian power and wealth.

In a daring land offensive, Sparta marched quickly to the borders of Athenian territory. Pericles, the Athenian leader at the time, called on all citizens living outside the city walls to move in. Summer temperatures rose as thousands of people crammed into small spaces in makeshift tents—and a plague struck. Athenians thought the disease arrived by ship from Ethiopia via Egypt.

Healthy individuals, including Thucydides, fell ill suddenly, starting with a headache followed by inflamed eyes, throat, and tongue. People nearby noticed that sufferers' breath stank. Soon the victims began sneezing, and they developed throaty hoarseness followed by a harsh cough. Next came terrible vomiting and retching.

Although the sufferers did not feel hot to the touch, they broke out in a skin rash and felt so hot inside they often tore off their clothes. Some ran outside stark naked looking for cold water to jump into. With unquenchable thirst, the sick cried out for drink. The disease worked its way through the body and down to the bowels. Many victims died with wild diarrhea after seven or eight days.

Of those who recovered, some lost eyesight, fingers, toes, and even memory, not knowing themselves or their friends. Thucydides noticed that families and helpers of the sick got sick,

too. Many victims were left to die alone in their homes or on the streets.

The Spartans did not attack Athens—they watched the black smoke of funeral pyres from outside the walls, too afraid to enter. The plague raged on and off for several years, killing over one-quarter of Athenians—including their leader, Pericles.

The experts at the 1999 medical conference came to the conclusion that typhus probably caused the Plague of Athens. Typhus usually hits in times of war and great hardship and lasts about seven days. Approximately one in five of its victims die. The disease is spread by the bite of an infected human body louse, a small parasite that flourishes in the warmth of people's armpits and groins when they do not change clothes or bathe.

Typhus causes dehydration with thirst, weakness, and—in some cases—a complication that leads to rotting fingers and toes. Other symptoms include high fever, red spots, and foul breath. Even though victims of typhus do not usually suffer extreme vomiting, diarrhea, memory loss, or blindness, typhus seemed to be the most likely choice.

Since the conference, workers discovered a burial pit in Athens that dates from about 430 BC. The bodies were stacked without soil between them, suggesting that the dead were dumped in the mass grave in a panic. DNA samples from the teeth show that the people suffered from typhoid fever, not typhus.

Typhoid fever is a disease linked to poor sanitation and hygiene—it is spread through food or drinking water that has come in contact with the feces of an infected person. Symptoms include high fever, headache, cough, diarrhea, rash of rose spots, and mental confusion. They do not include sneezing, bad breath, blindness, or rotting fingers and toes.

Of course, the Plague of Athens could have been a combination of two plagues—or three—raging at once in those cramped wartime conditions. The true answer may never be known.

Plague: a Word with Punch

The word "plague" comes from the Greek word *plaga* which means "strike" or "blow." Whatever the actual disease, the Plague of Athens was a whacking blow to the people of that ancient Greek city state.

Death of a Demigod

A thirty-two-year-old male, previously in good health, presented with high fever and acute pain in his abdomen. He had been drinking alcohol heavily for thirty-six hours and collapsed. Despite continuous fever, trouble sleeping, and weakness, the patient was able to eat, take baths, perform his religious duties, and meet with visitors for a number of days.

But on the seventh day, he worsened: his fever increased and he became so weak he needed assistance walking. On the ninth day, the patient was unable to sit up or speak but seemed to recognize his friends. He fell into a coma and died on the eleventh day of his illness.

Alexander the Great, King of Macedon and conqueror of Greece, Persia, Egypt, and the whole known world, died in Babylon just before his thirty-third birthday in June 323 BC.

This imaginary case history of Alexander's final days captures the mystery of his illness, but it leaves out some details that the scribes of his time included in their reports. No modern case history would include them—they seem too far-fetched to be possible.

One scribe claimed that a flock of ravens appeared overhead and started to fight in the sky as Alexander approached Babylon just before he fell sick. Several ravens dropped dead in front of him. Other scribes noted that Alexander's corpse did not decompose for several days after he died—even though it had been left in a hot, airless room. These details, however strange they seem, may hold clues to the cause of Alexander's death.

Soon after his death, people started to whisper that Alexander had been poisoned. After all, the world conqueror had many enemies. However, modern experts agree that poisons known at the time would not cause sudden pain followed by persistent fever for so many days. There is no record of vomiting, which usually accompanies overdrinking, so death by alcohol poisoning is unlikely.

Alexander probably died of an infectious disease, possibly blackwater fever, typhoid fever, or something like West Nile virus, which was not documented until modern times.

Blackwater fever is a fatal form of malaria that attacks not only the liver and blood but also the brain. A large swamp lay east of Ancient Babylon, located south of modern Baghdad on the shores of the Euphrates River. The area harbors malarial mosquitoes now and probably did in Alexander's time. Malaria would account for the high fever,

increasing weakness, inability to move, stupor, and coma. One unique symptom of blackwater fever is dark urine, but this is not mentioned in any records that describe Alexander's condition.

One rare complication of typhoid fever is a paralysis that creeps from the victim's feet to head. Sufferers breathe shallowly and fall into a coma, making it hard to tell when they have died because their chests do not seem to rise and fall as they breathe. Typhoid fever would explain Alexander's persistent fever and increasing weakness, but it would normally also present with cough, rash, and diarrhea, which are not mentioned. Typhoid fever also spreads in epidemics, but no major epidemic is reported at this time. Hephaestion, Alexander's best friend, however, also died of an unidentified disease around the same time.

West Nile Virus is a mosquito-borne illness. Infected mosquitoes pass this disease to birds—particularly members of the crow family, including ravens— and sometimes humans. People develop high fever, weakness, and inflammation of the brain, which can lead to paralysis, coma, and death.

This disease is not known to have existed in ancient times. In fact, it was first isolated in a human in 1937 in Africa. Today, people monitor unexplained bird deaths, especially members of the crow family, to determine if the virus is active locally. In ancient times, fortune-tellers observed bird behavior to predict the future—in Alexander's case, they just may have been right.

After his generals recovered from the shock of Alexander's death, they divided up his empire. They embalmed Alexander's body in honey, placed it in a gold coffin, and sent it off to Macedon. Then Ptolemy, the general who took charge in Egypt, hijacked the funeral procession. Ptolemy placed Alexander's body on display in the city of Alexandria at the mouth of the Nile River. About five hundred years later, an earthquake shattered parts of that city and Alexander's body disappeared. With no body, modern testing cannot determine his true cause of death.

Alexander himself had a theory. On the day of his death, Alexander apparently said, "I am dying from the treatment of too many physicians."

Empire and Epidemics

Could the most powerful empire in the ancient world collapse because of an epidemic—or two? After blaming the fall of Rome on barbarian invasions, too much corruption, or lead in the drinking water, historians now include epidemic disease as part of the equation.

At its height two thousand years ago, the Roman Empire circled the Mediterranean Sea—including modern-day Portugal and Spain, North Africa, the Middle East (including all of Turkey), most of central Europe, France, and parts of England. Less than a thousand years later, sheep and goats grazed among the crumbling Roman ruins.

The empire fell in two phases—both connected to epidemics.

Antonine Plague

In 165 AD, peoples north of the Danube River in Central Europe and those living east of Syria and Turkey pressed relentlessly against the boundaries of the Roman Empire. They wanted in—Rome held unimaginable riches as well as an iron grip over the ancient world. The Roman army stood firm, holding the boundaries against these "barbarians."

That year, soldiers campaigning in Seleucia, modern-day Iraq, fell ill with a plague and carried it home to Rome. The city had never seen such an epidemic—and it lasted fifteen years. At its height, two thousand people died every day. Bodies were stacked in the streets. The disease spread north and west, decimating the legions of soldiers stationed along the Danube and Rhine Rivers. In all, about five million people died—one out of every four who had been infected.

Aelius Galenus, known as Galen of Pergamon, a Greek physician and writer, was practicing medicine in Rome when the plague first struck. He did not catch the illness, but he described symptoms of fever, diarrhea, sore throat, and a rash—sometimes dry and sometimes forming pustules—that appeared on the ninth day. Although the details are few, the summary includes enough information for historians to guess that it was smallpox.

Marcus Aurelius Antoninus, a Roman emperor, wrote that the plague was less deadly than falsehood, evil behavior, and lack of understanding. In his last days before dying of the plague in 180 AD, Antoninus said, "Weep not for me—think rather of the pestilence and the deaths of so many others."

The plague reappeared in Rome in 251 AD and raged another twenty years, this time killing up to five thousand people a day, including Claudius, another Roman emperor. One historian wonders if this second plague marks the first appearance of measles in Europe, but most agree that it was a recurrence of smallpox.

The Antonine Plague shook Rome and the ancient world to its core. The Roman Empire never recovered from the second outbreak. In 285 AD, the empire split into east and west, with Rome as the western capital and Constantinople as the capital of the east. Over the next two hundred years, barbarians pressed closer to Rome until one horde sacked the city in 406 AD and another overran it totally in 476 AD.

Certainly moral decay and corruption ate into the boldness and courage of Rome, but this plague sapped its spirit and the strength of the people until collapse was inevitable.

The Plague of Justinian

In 542 AD, emperor Justinian of Constantinople, modern-day Istanbul, prepared to take back the western empire. His armies had already gained ground on the Italian peninsula and taken the city of Rome from Goth invaders from the north. Then a plague hit.

Citizens believed the plague came from Ethiopia via Egypt. Many were convinced it entered their homes through dreams or in visions of a headless stranger. Emperor Justinian, who fell ill with the disease but survived, commanded that the gates to the city be closed in an attempt to keep the epidemic out. Terrified, many citizens locked their own doors against strangers—and even family and friends. For most sufferers, the pain was intense and death came within a week of first feeling sick.

At its height in Constantinople, at least ten thousand people died every day. The emperor ordered all victims buried. When graveyards in and outside the city filled up, bodies were stacked and sealed inside towers in the walls of the city.

Eventually, corpses were loaded onto boats and set adrift with the sea current. At first, the keepers of the city gates kept track of the number

of corpses. They stopped counting at 230,000. The plague circled the Mediterranean Sea and spread into Europe, returning over and over again for about two hundred years. Modern doctors think that one-third of the population died in that epidemic.

Survivors understood that the plague was contagious. But because caregivers of the sick didn't necessarily get sick themselves, they suspected that the disease did not spread directly from person to person. Today, historians think this epidemic was likely bubonic plague, spread from the bite of an infected flea that lived on the rats that infested the city grain stores, homes, and alleyways.

Where did the disease come from originally? Perhaps from rodent colonies in Africa at the source of the Nile River, in the foothills of the Himalaya Mountains, or on the grassy plains of Russia east of Ukraine.

The Plague of Justinian marked a turning point in history. The ancient classical world disappeared and the Dark Ages descended on Europe. Cities shriveled, trade collapsed, and people moved back to the countryside.

In Constantinople, Justinian's dream of reuniting the Roman Empire failed. A northern people called the Lombards invaded and settled much of the Italian peninsula. The armies of Persia and then of Islam took over the eastern empire. The bubonic plague slumbered—but only for six hundred years.

Hippocrates and Galen— Miasmas and Humors vs the Supernatural

You're about to dash out to meet friends when your mom warns, "Don't forget a hat. You don't want to catch a chill." In Imperial Rome, your mom might have said, "Did you check the stars and signs, my child? Don't go out if they bode ill." And in ancient Greece, she might have asked, "Have you made your offerings yet? You don't want to provoke the gods and make us all sick."

Admit it—even though you know that microbes cause chills, sometimes you want to play it safe and stuff a hat in your pocket, say a prayer, or cross your fingers.

Hippocrates and the Greeks

Hippocrates was the first to challenge the ancient belief that disease is caused by supernatural forces. Born on the island of Cos, Greece, about 460 BC, Hippocrates and his followers wrote that a person's health can be understood by studying the natural world. A doctor, he claimed, helps a patient get well by observing the patient in his or her environment and by using reason.

Hippocrates developed the theory that good health came with balance among the four humors, or bodily fluids: blood, yellow bile, black bile, and phlegm. An excess of one humor upset the balance and caused illness. Too much phlegm, or mucus, for example, may cause a winter's cold— or too much yellow bile a bout of summer diarrhea. Black bile was associated with insanity—melancholy and mania. Blood was the hot life force, so cutting red meat from the diet or even starving a patient helped reduce fever.

Hippocrates noticed that people who lived near swamps often contracted malaria, so he deduced that malaria was caused by bad air expelled from swamp water. He used the term *miasma* to describe the fetid air of standing water, rotting flesh, and garbage.

Hippocrates's theories were not all correct. But he did advise doctors to put their patients first, make them comfortable, and respond carefully to observed symptoms—all cornerstones of modern medicine.

Many other ancient Greeks held on to the old belief that the plague was punishment by wrathful gods—after all, the Spartans outside Athens's walls were mostly spared. Even Alexander the Great, a highly educated man who had probably read Hippocrates's teachings, is said to have spent part of his last days sacrificing to the gods. Was this his daily religious duty or was he playing it safe? Maybe both.

Galen and imperial Rome

Galen of Pergamon was born in 129 AD in the eastern Roman Empire, modern-day Turkey. Although he lived over five hundred years after Hippocrates, Galen embraced many of Hippocrates's theories, including humors and miasmas.

A slick surgeon, Galen won a competition to become doctor to the gladiators in Turkey. He publicly cut out the bowels of a live ape, challenged his rivals to save the ape's life, and—when none dared—he sewed the creature back together himself.

His surgeries on wounded gladiators allowed him to explore inside the human body a little, which was otherwise forbidden in his time. Later, in Rome, he performed public autopsies on animals to impress the crowds and attract new patients. A favorite trick of his was to sever, one by one, the nerves in the neck of a squealing piglet until he severed the nerve to the voice box and the wretched piglet could no longer squeal.

Galen elaborated on Hippocrates's theory of the humors. He ordered vigorous bloodletting to cool a fever. Depending on the illness, blood could be drawn until the patient fainted. He recommended herb-induced diarrhea for symptoms such as swollen feet, and he encouraged sailing in stormy spring seas to induce vomiting for obesity.

His practices of bloodletting and purging—ideas that are crazy to us now—were followed for eighteen hundred years. They replaced the older traditions of astrology and divination, looking for signs and omens in the stars and animal world.

Galen was in Rome when the Antonine Plague struck. He recorded its symptoms and left shortly thereafter. He returned four years later, in 169 AD, when emperors Marcus Aurelius and Lucius Verus ordered him to take the position of court physician. Although both emperors died of the plague, Galen remained in Rome as personal physician to Marcus's son and heir, Emperor Commodus.

When he left Rome at the height of the plague, his enemies accused him of running away from the epidemic. Did he really believe that his methods to balance the humors would protect him from getting sick? Or was he playing it safe, too?

Many of the practices of Hippocrates and Galen survived the collapse of the ancient world. Some, such as bloodletting and forced vomiting, were considered good medicine until the nineteenth century. Putting patients first, taking careful patient histories, and doing no harm remain standards of care today. If you believe that clean, fresh air and a balanced life will prolong good health—you are following the teachings of these ancient doctors.

When your mom warns against catching a chill, do you put that hat on your head? If a really bad bug is going around, do you whisper a wish or say a little prayer? Old stories and theories are part of us all. There is comfort in ancient wisdom—and usually no harm.

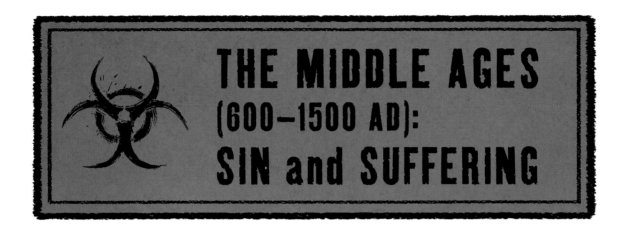

THE MIDDLE AGES (600–1500 AD): SIN and SUFFERING

Leprosy: The Wages of Sin

You've slipped back in time 800 years and find yourself standing on a dusty, rutted thoroughfare outside a hilltop town in central Italy. Below, you see travelers slowly trudging uphill, pausing at the sharp switchbacks. Some haul carts of vegetables or chickens in cages. A few lead squealing black pigs with sticks. Most carry one pack and hustle along with a staff.

The early morning sun warms your face. It's a pleasant feeling—until a woman wearing a shawl and flowing skirts passes by, using a rope to drag a goat behind her. The goat's intense, musky tang irritates your nose.

You watch one figure limping up on your side of the path. When others overtake him, they swerve wide to pass. He's barefoot and dressed in just a few rags over his shoulders and around his waist, with bandage strips on his head.

An annoying clanging noise gets louder as he approaches. Now you see a bell in his hand. He lifts his head and you look into his young face.

Thick, scaly skin bulges and furrows along his eyebrows and chin. His nose looks like a punched-in, star-shaped dimple. The skin on his arms and legs is crusty, and oozing sores disfigure his feet. He approaches you, pushes forward an empty cup with pleading eyes. Stubby claws for fingers curl around the cup's rim. He smells of dust and sweat and wet soil.

Someone hisses, "Unclean!" And you are pulled sharply away. The cupbearer looks scared and twists his body, expecting a blow.

What do you feel? Are you scared for him, for you, or for what you don't know?

Leprosy is an ancient disease. Lepers were shunned from early times in China, India, and Africa, then the Middle East and Europe, and now around the world. Even though today leprosy is curable with drugs, most people remain ignorant of the disease and—filled with old fears and superstitions—recoil from its victims.

We now know that leprosy is a bacterium probably transmitted in airborne droplets from a sneeze or cough. The disease attacks the muscles and nerves in the cooler parts of the body—skin, eyes, nose, hands, and feet.

Without proper early treatment, the disease leaves disfiguring scars. Muscles stiffen so that fingers twist and shorten into claws. Feet become rigid and curled, sometimes flopping at the ankle and making it impossible to walk normally. Muscles in the eyelids fail so that victims cannot blink and slowly go blind. Numbness develops in the legs and arms, which means that sufferers can become injured without feeling it. With no pain, wounds can go unnoticed and untreated leading to dangerous infections that require amputations.

The first known case of leprosy occurred about four thousand years ago; the disease was discovered in a skeleton in India. Historians believe a virulent strain was carried back to the Middle East with Alexander the

Hansen's Disease

In 1873, Gerhard Armauer Hansen of Norway discovered the bacterium that causes leprosy.

Norway? At the time, Norway and Iceland were the only countries in Europe where leprosy was a growing problem. Leprosy became a hot political issue, and the government provided extra resources to learn more about the disease. Hansen's discovery was initially discredited by other doctors, including his father-in-law, who were sure the disease was genetic and hereditary.

It took a long time to find a cure. From the early twentieth century until the 1940s, the best-known treatment was an injection of oil from the chaulmoogra nut. Today, doctors use long-term multi-drug treatments to stop the disease from disfiguring the patient and from infecting others. Researchers still look for a vaccination and for ways to detect the disease in its first stages.

To kill the age-old stigma against leprosy victims, advocates have successfully lobbied to change the medical name from leprosy to Hansen's disease. But the word leprosy lingers—people still whisper it and imagine a living death.

Great's army about 324 BC. From there, it slowly spread to Europe with the movements of Roman armies and eventually the Crusades. In biblical times and the early Middle Ages, leprosy was confused with other disfiguring skin diseases—even out-of-control dandruff.

Sometime after 1000 AD, leprosy reached pandemic proportions in Europe. People feared they could catch it by simple touch. Some believed that God inflicted leprosy on a person as a punishment for the sin of lust.

In 1179, a council of the Catholic church declared that lepers must be separated from society. A special mass pronounced individual lepers legally dead. Forbidden to marry, stripped of their belongings, lepers were refused burial in church cemeteries. They were required to carry a bell or clapper, wear distinctive clothing, walk on a certain side of the road (depending on the winds), and sleep outside of town.

Compassionate Christians argued that lepers live in a place of suffering between life and death on Earth—and that when they die, lepers go straight to heaven. Helping lepers came to be seen

as a route to holiness. Monks and nuns set up leprosariums, or hospitals for lepers. Townspeople eventually joined the cause. There were nineteen thousand leprosariums in Europe by 1225.

Around 1350, the leprosy pandemic collapsed. At first, historians thought the decline was caused by the appearance of the Black Death plague. However, it's now believed that the tuberculosis microbe, a bacterium quite similar to leprosy, elbowed leprosy out. The leprosariums became shelters for new outcasts—victims of plague, insanity, and homelessness.

Leprosy still exists today. In fact, a child is diagnosed with leprosy every twenty minutes. But it is curable— when victims don't hide for shame and can find medical help.

The Black Death (1348–1351)

What does the Mongolian marmot have to do with one of the worst pandemics ever?

In the early Middle Ages, native people living on the high grasslands of Central Asia trapped large rodents called Mongolian marmots to eat the meat and sell the furs. When these hunters found dead marmots lying about on the land, they moved on to find healthy colonies. They believed it was bad luck to camp near dead marmots. Bad luck, indeed—marmot colonies could act as reservoirs of bubonic plague. Even today, the disease can flare up unexpectedly among Mongolian marmots and the fleas that bite them.

In the early 1300s, when traveling Chinese merchants came across colonies of Mongolian marmots lying dead or dying, they thought they'd hit the jackpot. Despite the customs of local people, the outsiders skinned the marmots to sell the valuable pelts along caravan routes to the east, south, and west.

When the merchants opened the fur bales at their destinations, starving infected fleas jumped out looking for a blood meal—and fast. No marmots to feed on? To a rodent flea, black rat blood tastes just as good. And at that time, black rats overran the gutters, granaries, and homes of Asian, Middle Eastern, North African, and European towns.

The bite of one infected flea into the skin of one black rat may be how the bubonic plague returned and then spread through the Old World in the Middle Ages, killing tens of millions of people. At first, this bubonic plague pandemic was called the Great

Pestilence, but it soon became known as the Black Death.

A person gets the disease when a rodent—usually a rat—dies of the plague and one of its infected fleas, hungry for its next blood meal, can only find a human to bite. Humans are a second choice to rats. An infected flea bites over and over again because its gut clogs with bacteria, making its hunger and thirst endless. Gorged but ravenous, the flea even vomits its meal of blood back into its victim and drinks again. They are like living syringes of disease.

A victim of bubonic plague first notices flu-like symptoms with sudden fever, headache, back pain, and soreness in the arms and legs. Within a day or two, painful swellings, or buboes, appear in the groin and sometimes in the armpits, on the thighs, and the neck.

Each bubo, at first rosy and smooth but always painful and burning, grows to the size of an egg—or even an apple. The skin circling the base of the bubo turns dark, and finally the bubo blackens. Buboes can burst open and ooze blood and pus. Later symptoms include a rash of black blisters, restlessness, and delirium. Black blotches cover the body as blood pools under the skin. In some cases, urine, vomit, and diarrhea all turn black and putrid.

From Asia to Europe

In 1346, Mongol warriors attacked and blockaded the town of Caffa, modern-day Feodosiya, Ukraine, on the north shore of the Black Sea. Behind the walls, the governor and traders from Genoa, Italy, hunkered down to wait out the siege.

But outside, the attackers started dying from bubonic plague. In a desperate move, as their numbers decimated, the Mongols catapulted corpses over the town walls, hoping the Genoese would catch the disease, too—and give up. But the plague overwhelmed the Mongols first, and they had to retreat.

Terrified, the Genoese traders dashed to their boats and set sail for Italy. But black rats infested their boats. The trail back to Genoa was littered with death—people and rats.

Tuscany, italy

When the boats docked in Italy, the plague exploded in the rat-infested seaports and then spread inland. The city of Florence, a wealthy trading center in Tuscany, took one of the worst hits. By the end of 1348, half its population lay dead. Giovanni

Boccaccio, a local author, quipped, "How many valiant men, how many fair ladies breakfasted with their kinsfolk and the same night supped with their ancestors...."

Boccaccio also wrote that a sick person could pass on the disease just by walking past someone healthy. This suggests that some Florentines suffered a dreadful form of the bubonic plague—one called pneumonic plague, which spreads human to human by a cough or sneeze from infected lungs.

Because the disease seemed to attack anyone in the city, rich or poor, people reasoned it must spread through the air that everyone breathed. So the citizens went about their business holding handfuls of fresh aromatic herbs to their noses and adding fragrant wood to outdoor bonfires, desperately believing the sweet smells would cleanse the foulness in the air.

A few of the rich left the city for their country villas. The outlying areas proved safer, and many in the countryside survived. But the problem was not the air in the city—it was the architecture. City houses were designed with grain storage on the ground floor

and living space upstairs. Infected rats fed on the grain downstairs and then ran up into people's personal lives.

Stories circulated of neighbors bricking up entire homes, sealing inside whole families known to be nursing the sick. Boccaccio, whose father died of the plague, angrily accused the doctors of charging high prices while offering no effective cure. In Florence, undertakers hired to carry away the dead were accused of being heartless, even robbing or murdering victims.

So many people died that crops lay untended in the fields. Plague survivors suffered starvation, adding to the death toll. In nearby Siena, labor stopped on renovations to the cathedral because too many craftsmen died—and that building remains unfinished today.

Western Europe

The plague raced toward France, Germany, and the Netherlands. People waited in dread.

Most of the cats in Europe were tabbies, a breed that comes in various shades of striped brown. Black cats were rare in Europe but common in the Middle East. When Europeans saw

black cats in their neighborhoods, they panicked, assuming if black cats were present, so was the plague because both came on ships from the east. People decided to kill all black cats, and soon town councils were ordering every dog and cat destroyed to prevent plague—the very animals that might naturally control the rat population.

Meanwhile, groups of frantic poor people roamed from town to town, whipping each other in public, preaching, and loudly confessing their sins to God. They called themselves the Flagellants, from a Latin word meaning "to whip." They hoped their pain would appease God's wrath so they would be spared the plague. In a few towns, the Flagellants worked themselves into such a frenzy that they turned against innocent Jews whom they blamed for spreading the plague. In 1349, in the German cities of Mainz, Strasbourg, and then Frankfurt, the Flagellants slaughtered thousands of Jews. In Basel, Switzerland, they forced Jews into wooden buildings and burned them alive. Pope Clement VI finally banned the Flagellant movement later that year.

Some town councils stationed guards at their gates and refused entry to those from plague-stricken areas. But merchants used vinegar to erase offending town names on their travel documents. Other town councils worried that news of plague was bad for business, and they lied about the numbers of sick and dead. Of course, this forging, smuggling, and covering up only helped spread the Black Death.

When the bubonic plague reached Vienna, Austria, in 1349, people were sure it was the result of strange natural events—a recent eclipse of the sun, an earthquake, severe rainstorms, unusually warm weather, devastating fires, and swarms of locusts.

Reports are scarce, but it's known that—unlike Florence—even the rich Viennese stayed in the city, prayed hard, and donated generously to the church to pay for masses in memory of the dead. Deaths rates were highest among the poor and the gravediggers.

Northern Europe

The plague raced north. In Scotland, the poor families living in their thatch huts died in larger numbers than the rich living in their stone mansions—rats like to bed down in straw, the same material used for making thatch roofs.

Half the population of Norway died after a boatload of dead sailors drifted into Bergen. The boat had set sail from England with a healthy crew, a cargo of wool, and stowaway rats, but the sailors sickened before they reached their destination. The plague circled east into Russia by 1351, and it headed back south toward Caffa, where the pandemic began only five years before.

The Black Death moved so fast and with such devastation that some scientists wonder if it was more than bubonic plague—maybe a mixture of smallpox and bubonic plague that fed each other in some horrible way. But recent research has shown that the DNA of the microbe that caused the Black Death is the same as the microbe that causes the isolated cases of bubonic plague that appear in modern times. The speed and severity of the Black Death probably had more to do with the way people lived—in close company with rats—than with the genetics of the disease.

Today, in Mongolia, people avoid colonies of unhealthy marmots because they still harbor bubonic plague. In a strange twist of fate, Mongolian marmots are now listed as an endangered species—not because of bubonic plague, but because they have been overhunted for their fur.

Living with Death

BOO!

When kids feel scared, they make up games to laugh at their fear. It's a natural way to control something that's beyond control.

Perhaps the old nursery rhyme and circle game "Ring around the Rosie" helped kids overcome their fear of bubonic plague. Some historians think it was invented in the Middle Ages for just that reason!

Ring around the rosie,
A pocket full of posy,
Husha, husha,
We all fall down.

Remember this poem—or a variation of it? While chanting the verse in a singsong voice, kids hold hands and turn in a circle together. At the end of the last line, everyone drops hands and falls to the ground.

If you read the poem line by line, you will see that it seems to describe the course of bubonic plague. The buboes swell up and become a rosy color while the skin circling them turns into dark rings. People carried sweet-smelling posies of herbs for protection. "Husha, husha" mimics the last gasping rattle in the throat before death. Finally, the disease knocked most people down ... dead!

Certainly, the bubonic plague was scary. It raced around the known world once and then it returned again and again for over four hundred years. Each generation experienced waves of sickness and death. With no known cure, a circle game was as good as any other way of coping.

People tried all kinds of crazy treatments to deal with the plague such as starving, eating sugar candy, spraying buboes with snake poison or vinegar, and applying pepper or plucked chicken rumps to the sores.

Medical treatments prescribed by doctors were useless. They included forced vomiting, bloodletting, and lancing the buboes to release pus—which usually just made matters worse and spread bacteria. Some people believed that herbal mixtures were the answer—such as lavender, marjoram, cloves, and cinnamon—to be added to hot soup, held up to the nose, rubbed on the skin, or carried in a pocket.

In Italy, doctors wore a uniform when visiting the sick. Before plague times, the uniform was a red cloak trimmed with white fur, a bit like Santa Claus. In plague times, they dressed in dark leather cloaks, wore gloves, and fastened beak-like white masks over their mouth and nose. They stuffed herbs inside the "beak" so that they could inhale healthy fragrances while keeping both hands free to carry the sticks they used to push back the sick who pressed too close.

Eventually, communities started to take responsibility for public health. In 1377, the town councillors of Ragusa, modern-day Dubrovnik in Croatia, isolated boats and crew before any sailors were allowed to come ashore. Other ports followed their lead, adopting forty-day quarantines.

By 1450 in France, keepers of town gates routinely inspected travelers' documents to be sure no one entered who had recently passed through an infected area—watching

orphans. In Florence, the town so many rich people had left in the first wave, a Book of the Dead was created to remember the names of the victims. During an outbreak in 1630, the Grand Duke of Tuscany made daily rounds of the city of Florence to be sure his people were well cared for.

In the early eighteenth century, the bubonic plague finally vanished from Europe, but not before two deadly recurrences that coincided with shipments of fabric probably swarming with fleas. The Great Plague of London, England, which began in 1665 and lasted a year, may be linked to infested bales of cotton from the Netherlands that were offloaded from ships in the dock area. At its height, seven thousand people died every week in London. People started small fires all over town to purify the air. The London plague ended in 1666 when the older part of city, including the rat-infested slums, went up in flames.

Children and adults remembered these terrifying years in a little ditty. Their horror may have been eased by downplaying their troubles into a few flippant words.

In 1665, no one was left alive.
In 1666, London was burned to sticks.

for forgeries. In Scotland, by the mid-1500s, authorities transported plague victims out of town and provided them with special huts to live in. Corpses had to be buried at least seven feet deep, huts cleaned, and bedding boiled before reuse.

As the years went by, more European towns allocated money to construct isolation hospitals, hire doctors and nurses, and care for

The second serious plague outbreak linked to a shipment of fabric occurred in 1720. Almost half the population of Marseilles, France, died over the next two years, starting with the sailors, porters, and buyers of a boatload of cloth from Syria.

The plague flared up a few more times in smaller towns and then disappeared mysteriously for a hundred years.

The Art of Death

Visit a three-hundred-year-old cemetery in Spain and you may see a skull and crossbones carved over the gate. Nothing to do with pirates, nothing to do with toxic household products, but the same icon. Today, we'd consider this a weird decoration for a graveyard, but survivors of the bubonic plague liked to be reminded of the meaning of death.

Connecting the Bites

In the late nineteenth century, bubonic plague broke out again in the Far East. Dr. Alexandre Yersin, a French scientist, was stationed there as a physician at the time. He set up shop outside a plague hospital in Hong Kong and examined the corpses of plague victims. In 1894, he was able to isolate the plague bacterium, which is now named after him— *Yersinia pestis*.

Paul-Louis Simond, a fellow Frenchman, made the connection between Yersin's bacterium and fleas on rats four years later. Ever since the Middle Ages, people had known that an unusually high number of dead rats appeared in gutters just before a flare-up of plague. There was even a name for it—a ratfall. Simond and his colleagues discovered that rats in a ratfall died of bubonic plague. Then Simond noticed marks like insect bites on the skin of human victims.

In 1898, he conducted an experiment. He put one rat infected with the plague in a cage, and he placed an uninfected rat in another cage. Then he put the two cages close together—but not touching. He introduced uninfected fleas to the experiment and soon both rats had plague. The fleas had caught the disease from the sick rat and passed it on to the healthy one. Yersin's and Simond's sharp eyes and curious minds solved the riddle of the bubonic plague. As Simond pointed out, it's hard to believe that such a simple answer—controlling rat populations— could have saved millions of lives.

In 1897, Dr. Waldemar Haffkine, a Russian working in India, created the first vaccine against bubonic plague. Today, only people who work with infected laboratory animals need to be vaccinated because the disease is curable with antibiotics. The plague still simmers in rodent colonies around the world—including in colonies of ground squirrels in the American Southwest.

Enter a chapel in an old European church and you might come across a life-size statue of a skeleton lying on a raised tomb, with worms crawling in the eye sockets and rib cage. What's even more amazing—this is serious art, worked in fine polished marble. These cadaver monuments, often carefully planned by powerful citizens before they died, were popular for a short time in the late 1300s and early 1400s. Sudden, painful death was so common in bubonic plague times that death's gory details made their way into the art of the time.

In the 1400s and 1500s, European artists created works of art that depicted Death and humans in a *Danse Macabre*. Representatives from all levels in society—pope, king, bishop, knight, merchant, peasant, beggar, and child—formed a line. Sprightly skeletons slipped in between each and all held hands. The dance began—the living humans trudging along with downcast eyes while the skeletons leaped with glee. Of course, the skeletons escorted all their dance partners to their deaths.

In England, some artists imagined Death as a skeleton, now known as the grim reaper, wearing a black hooded cape and carrying a scythe. In other countries, a similar spirit wore motley clothes or appeared as a fiendish hag or pale horseman—all depictions led people from this world to the next. Some people believed you could enter a game of wits with Death, and—if you won—be awarded a longer life.

The Pied Piper

The fairy tale called "The Pied Piper of Hamelin" carries echoes of these Death images. Although parts of the tale refer to events that occurred before the plague, the story of a rat-catching pied piper first appeared in bubonic plague years.

In the version recorded about 1550, the town of Hamelin, Germany, is overrun with rats. A stranger wearing an outlandish, multicolored costume and carrying a musical pipe offers to get rid of the rats for a fee. The merchants agree and the stranger starts to play an unusual tune. The rats, enchanted, follow him to the river where they all drown.

When the piper asks for his money, the merchants won't pay him. Why should they pay a fee for such an easy job? The piper warns them that they will regret it if they don't pay, but the merchants shrug him off, believing he can cause them no harm.

So the piper leaves the city and returns in a green huntsman's costume, still carrying his pipe. He plays his instrument again, but this time, the town's children follow. Mesmerized, they dance along behind him and disappear into a mountain cave. Only three children survive—one deaf, one blind, and one lame—because they can't keep up with the rest.

Does the pied piper, in his strange costume and with supernatural powers, lead a *Danse Macabre*?

Iconic Saints

Paintings of Saint Sebastian and Saint Roch, darkened with age and caked with soot, still hang in some old European churches. Worshippers lit candles and prayed to these saints for protection in plague times.

Saint Sebastian is usually shown tied to a pole, his face contorted in agony, his body pierced through by arrows. People believed that bad air carried the plague, but—if it passed through the piercings in Saint Sebastian's body—the air became purified.

Saint Roch is always painted with buboes on his thigh and in the company of a dog. He apparently caught the plague in the wilderness and survived because a dog brought him food. People sought Saint Roch's protection by praying, lighting candles, and carrying his icon in procession through infected towns.

Ironically, the popular custom of going on pilgrimages, processions, and crusades—meant to please and serve God or saints—spread plague and other diseases to new areas.

So You Think You Can Dance?

Watching your parents dance together—fast or slow—can be embarrassing, even if they are really accomplished performers. For a time in the Middle Ages, between the thirteenth and seventeenth centuries, kids had a lot of dancing to watch—and it was bizarre.

Outbreaks of an illness called the dancing mania possessed townsfolk, especially the poor. Those afflicted danced themselves to exhaustion—even death—in the streets. Was it the dance of death? It was considered contagious at the time, but was it really a disease?

Screaming, singing, crying, and laughing maniacally, the affected jerked their bodies as if they were having seizures. Some wore strange costumes and decorated their hair with garlands, some became violent when they saw the color red, some pulled off their clothes and made obscene gestures, and some crawled in the dirt like animals. The dancers gyrated, howled, and wept for hours, even days. Occasionally they danced together by the thousands, growing in numbers as they roamed from town to town.

Bystanders joined in or watched from a safe distance. Was this madness, sickness, or religious ecstasy? Eventually, the frenzied dancers would fall down in mass exhaustion: it was over. Some woke up and walked back into normal lives while others were possessed over and over again.

An early outbreak of dancing mania occurred in 1237, with a large group of children dancing between the German towns of Erfurt and Arnstadt. And in 1278, so many people danced on a bridge over the river Meuse, in Germany, that it collapsed into the water.

Most outbreaks, however, occurred after the beginning of the Black Death. In the summer of 1374, a group started dancing in Aachen, Germany, and the outbreak spread to nearby communities and then to surrounding countries—including France, the Netherlands, Belgium, and Italy.

In 1518, a woman called Frau Troffea started dancing alone in Strasbourg, Germany. After a month, over four hundred people had joined her—most died of stroke, exhaustion, and heart attack.

At the time, people believed that the best way to help the afflicted was to provide music. Pipers played quick-paced, upbeat tunes so the dancers could follow in a rhythmic pattern, sweat out what ailed them, and be cured—or so people thought. Priests asked the musicians to lead the throngs to chapels, where they might be blessed or exorcised and cured. Shrines to Saint Vitus were thought to be so helpful in curing the afflicted that the dancing mania became known as Saint Vitus's dance.

In southern Italy, where doctors believed that the dancers had been poisoned by tarantula bites, musicians played upbeat, hypnotic tunes called tarantellas to separate the poison from the blood. Tarantellas have worked their way into the folk music and dance tradition, accompanied today by tambourines.

In the seventeenth century, the dancing mania suddenly disappeared. What caused it and why did it vanish? No one really knows.

Some historians believe that the dancing mania was really Saint Anthony's fire, a disease that causes people to hallucinate and go crazy with a burning sensation in their arms and legs. Saint Anthony's fire is connected to eating rye flour infected by a fungus.

Another possibility is Sydenham's chorea, a disease in which patients suffer from involuntary muscle movements after a bout of rheumatic fever. But today, neither Saint Anthony's fire nor Sydenham's chorea causes the prolonged, strange behaviors of the dancers.

Perhaps the dancing mania was a form of mass hysteria brought on by the terrible stresses of poverty, hunger, and—most importantly—the Black Death. Or it may have been a movement totally misunderstood by onlookers at the time—could it have been teenagers and social outcasts going over the edge, Middle Ages–style?

We may never know what caused the dancing mania, but it would have been astonishing to watch.

The English Sweat

Epidemics set their own rules. They leap over fences, duck under searchlights, sneak through metal detectors, and slip past borders without an invitation, permission, or a passport.

In the late Middle Ages, a deadly epidemic hit England but stopped cold at the Scottish border. At the time, people found that strange … and people today do, too.

This epidemic struck five times between the years 1485 and 1551, always during the summer. Oddly, the disease never spread to Scotland or Wales, and the only victims in Ireland had been recent visitors to England. The disease once spread into continental Europe, but then it disappeared.

Called the English sweat, or the sweat, its unique symptom was violent, unstoppable, stinky sweating. Other symptoms included headache, fever, weakness, and death within hours.

Gallant young men were said to be dancing at nine o'clock, dead at eleven.

Although the sweat occurred at the same time as the bubonic plague, the unbelievably heavy, smelly sweating—with no buboes—distinguished it as a different illness. People also noticed that, unlike the plague, the sweat attacked country dwellers more often than those living in tightly packed cities. Rich, young men in the prime of their lives died more often than children, women, the elderly, and the poor. "Gallant" and "knave" were names used for carefree young men in the age-range most afflicted—a gallant being more stylish and brave than a knave who tended to be a rascal. The poor had two nicknames for the disease: the Stop Gallant! and the Stop Knave!.

The year 1485, the first summer the plague struck, coincided with Henry Tudor's defeat of King Richard III on the battlefield. People worried that the sweat was a form of punishment to the English for killing and replacing the anointed king with an upstart. But by late October, the English sweat had vanished, and Henry's coronation ushered in a new line of powerful kings and queens.

Each time the English sweat returned, it peaked during a warm, wet summer and disappeared with the autumn frost. Diseases today that are seasonal and that occur within precise geographical limits are usually passed from birds or rodents through insects to people. The insect that transmits the disease is called a vector. With the English sweat, the insect could have been a mosquito, fly, louse, or tick—of those, especially mosquitoes flourish in warm, wet summers and die off with frost. We don't know which bird or rodent acted as the host, but wood mice and voles lived in distinct habitat zones in England and either could easily have harbored the disease.

It's possible that the English sweat vanished because it was a virus that just burned itself out. Or maybe the English developed immunity to the sweat. Perhaps it mutated into something so mild that people didn't consider it a sickness anymore. Or maybe the bird or rodent host or the insect vector disappeared with the cutting down of the great forests in England.

By the time the English sweat occurred, the Middle Ages in Europe were already in decline and an age of exploration and discovery was beginning. Terrible plagues over the past two hundred years had forged many changes. Ordinary folk no longer supported their governments with unquestioning obedience or their church with blind faith. What use were kings and bishops when they couldn't stop the suffering?

The population in Europe fell dramatically. Workers were scarcer and demanded higher wages and more rights. With fewer people to farm the land, pasture for livestock replaced fields for crops. The old feudal system of knights and serfs disappeared, and a more powerful middle class was rising in towns.

Doctors in the year 1550 still had no real understanding of infectious disease—even though they were now observing distinctions between illnesses. Public health was in its infancy. Epidemics swept across borders and through communities while people watched helplessly … and prayed.

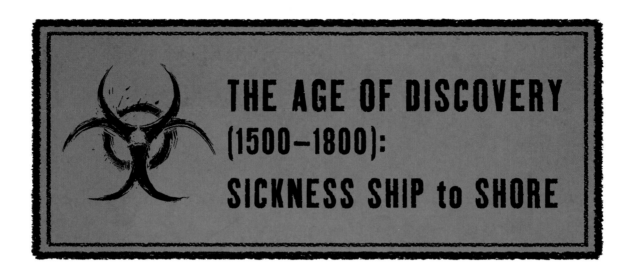

THE AGE OF DISCOVERY (1500–1800): SICKNESS SHIP to SHORE

Smallpox Goes Viral

Around the time Christopher Columbus sailed to the Americas in 1492, the number of smallpox cases spiked in Europe, Africa, and Asia. A killer from ancient times, the smallpox virus turned even more deadly. Three out of every ten people who caught it died—eight out of every ten children. In cities, smallpox returned so regularly—at least every twenty years—that the majority of adults were immune to the disease because they had survived a bout of it. Smallpox began to target young people who'd never been exposed and had no immunity. It became a dreaded childhood disease.

In the 1500s, no one understood what caused smallpox, how it was transmitted, that it was infectious before the rash appeared, that surviving one time meant lifelong immunity, how

to treat it, or how to prevent it. Doctors did understand, however, that smallpox was a distinct contagious disease—one commonly called the pox.

If you caught smallpox, you'd suddenly feel out of sorts twelve days after exposure. Your early symptoms would include flu-like fever, faintness, headache, backache, nausea, and weakness. After a day or two, you'd feel a little better. But then your fever would spike again, you'd get a splitting headache as well as a knife-stabbing pain in your back. By day four, minute red spots would erupt in your nose, mouth, and throat. Then the rash would appear on your forehead and face—distinctive, red spots—and spread throughout your mouth, throat, down your upper back, chest, arms, and legs. The spots turned into brownish

pustules—enlarged pimple-like bumps filled with milky fluid.

In bad cases of the pox, the pustules would spread over your eyeballs, your internal organs, and all your skin—including your scalp and the soles of your feet. The pustules in your mouth and throat would make drinking and eating difficult. With high fever and painful rash, patients often fell unconscious. Sometimes the pustules would grow inwards, hemorrhage, and bring early death. In horrific cases, the pustules would all run together and your rash-covered skin would separate from the underlying flesh, peeling off in sheets.

By day eleven, the pustules would flatten and then crust into scabs. Bacterial infection would often set in, adding a whole new set of complications. If you made it through the third week, when the scabs started to fall off, you survived. But your skin could be pockmarked with unsightly, white, indented scars, especially on your face. The scars would never disappear—you were marked for life—and you could be bald, blind, and infertile as well.

Does this sound like bad news? Not compared to what happened in the New World! Christopher Columbus brought the Old World to the New, including diseases. Within a few years, millions of Native Americans had died from smallpox. They got sicker faster—some died even before the pustules formed.

Contagion or Conquest? Old Diseases Meet New Peoples

In 1518, Hernán Cortés, a Spanish soldier stationed in Cuba, persuaded the island governor, Diego Velázquez, to let him explore the coast of Mexico. This sounded straightforward enough—but Cortés had a secret agenda. He hungered for gold. A conquistador at heart, he would do anything, even commit murder, to fill his pockets. But Cortés never intended to unleash a pandemic that caused the deaths of millions of people.

Cortés outfitted a fleet of ships with soldiers and cannons. Just before he set sail, the Cuban governor began to suspect Cortés's greed and cancelled his mission. Cortés sailed anyway. When he reached Mexico, he listened to the locals' stories about the fabulously wealthy Aztec Empire.

Cortés and a small army of soldiers marched inland to the Aztec capital, Tenochtitlán. When they reached the city, Emperor Montezuma welcomed them. The Spaniards were amazed. Tenochtitlán was home to more people and a greater number of massive monumental structures than Seville, Spain. The gold glittering on the buildings and people bedazzled Cortés and his men.

In no time, Cortés took Montezuma hostage and demanded the empire's gold as ransom. He also ordered that the Aztecs pledge allegiance to the Spanish king and accept the Christian god as their own. The Aztecs submitted, hoping to buy back Montezuma's freedom.

In the middle of the coup, Cortés suddenly had to race back to the coast to surprise a Spanish Cuban force that was intent on arresting him. After he succeeded and returned to Tenochtitlán, Cortés found Montezuma dead— probably killed by his own people. The Aztecs chose a new emperor and rebelled against the Spanish. Cortés, his troops, and his entourage retreated. Many of his men drowned, sinking in lakes and rivers with their heavy armor. One of the Spanish soldiers or

servants carried the smallpox virus—
and that's all it took to spread the
disease to the Aztecs.

Two years later, Cortés returned to
Tenochtitlán with a few hundred armed
men. After a siege, he broke into the
city and found half the population dead
from smallpox. His chronicler Bernal
Diaz wrote, "I solemnly swear that all
the houses and stockades in the lake
were full of heads and corpses ... We

could not walk without treading on the
bodies and heads of dead Indians."

The Aztec empire collapsed. As
more Spaniards swarmed the New
World searching for gold, they spread
wave after wave of European diseases—
smallpox, influenza, measles, scarlet
fever, and bubonic plague. Pandemics
raced ahead of the conquistadors—up
the Mississippi Valley and down into
South America.

Cortés and the Spanish believed that the death of so many was the will of God. In truth, the Native Americans died because they had no immunity to European diseases. These healthy peoples had lived in isolation from Europe and Asia for over ten thousand years. At the end of the last ice age, a land bridge between Siberia and Alaska flooded, cutting the Americas off from the Old World. Native Americans built their own civilizations, and—because they kept few domesticated animals—suffered few infectious diseases. Unlike Europeans, whose adult population carried a high resistance to smallpox, the Native Americans carried no resistance.

Thirteen years after the fall of Tenochtitlán, Spaniard Francisco Pizarro entered the Inca city of Cuzco in Peru. Smallpox was already killing the city's population. Smallpox had burned like wildfire through the thousands of miles of land between Mexico and Peru, devastating countless communities all along the way. Pizarro toppled and looted the powerful Inca Empire with only a few hundred men.

In chains, the emperor sneered at Pizarro. "Did the Spanish *eat* gold?" he wanted to know. Pizarro said yes, they did. Pizarro got his gold

not only because he was a clever, ruthless conquistador, but also because smallpox had decimated the Incas.

Over the next century when the English, French, Dutch, and Portuguese settled in the New World, they also spread disease. A few generations after the Puritans from England landed in Massachusetts and Connecticut, nine out of ten of the Narragansett and Mohawk peoples had died of smallpox, whooping cough, measles, influenza, or typhus. The Puritans thought they must be divinely favored because few of them died.

By 1645 in modern-day Ontario, the great Wendat nation was halved mostly by smallpox, but also scarlet fever, influenza, and measles—carried inland by Jesuit priests and fur traders. The story repeated itself over and over through the New World and then the South Pacific.

Smallpox flared up again with the sweeping movements of people during the American Revolution in 1776. After the war, smallpox reached the Pacific Coast, probably carried along native trading routes, decimating communities unknown to Europeans. When Captain George Vancouver of the British Royal Navy explored the Pacific Northwest in 1792, he found plentiful salmon and fresh water, but also deserted villages scattered with human bones—evidence of a recent catastrophe. Smallpox had left its scars.

North and South America may have been home to a hundred million people when Columbus, Cortés, and Pizarro appeared on their shores. Three centuries later, fewer than ten million remained.

Inoculation, Vaccination, Extinction

Hindus in India discovered a way to control smallpox over two thousand years ago. Old manuscripts describe how Brahman priests traveled the countryside rubbing bits of dried smallpox scabs into the cuts or scratches of people who had never had the disease.

A thousand years later in China, people self-inoculated by inhaling a powder of ground-up scabs from recovering smallpox patients. Both methods transmitted small doses of the virus, but the resulting illness tended to be mild. If the inoculated were kept in isolation for a while, the disease did not spread. No one understood why this worked—just that it did. The practice slowly extended throughout Asia, Africa, and into Turkey.

In 1715, the beautiful Lady Mary Wortley Montagu of England, at the age of 26, caught smallpox. She survived, but her twenty-two-year-old brother did not. Beautiful no more, Lady Mary looked into her mirror to see a face pitted with scars and no eyelashes. She traveled with her husband to Turkey, where she discovered inoculation.

Lady Mary researched the process carefully and was so impressed that she had her young daughter, age four, inoculated. Over the next few years, she persuaded the Princess of Wales to inoculate her children. Lady Mary and promoters of the procedure called it variolation after the medical name

Smallpox and Biological Warfare

Cortés may not have intended to spread smallpox in the Americas, but some Europeans did. In 1763, during the Seven Years War between the French and English to control the colonies, Sir Jeffrey Amherst asked his British troops to deliberately infect the Native American allies of the French. His officer in Pennsylvania agreed to smear blankets with the pus of active smallpox sores and distribute them among the native peoples. The ruse worked. Many Native Americans died, and eventually the English won.

for the disease (variola). They hoped to make inoculation popular.

About the same time in Boston, Massachusetts, Reverend Cotton Mather learned about inoculation from his African slave Onesimus. He persuaded a local physician to inoculate his patients, and together they were able to protect about 250 Bostonians during a smallpox outbreak in 1722.

Despite Lady Mary and Reverend Mather's successes, inoculation did not catch on quickly. In both England and the American colonies, local authorities were cautious of the procedure—it made no theoretical sense, didn't always work, and risked spread of the disease.

However, when smallpox reared its head partway through the American Revolution, George Washington, the first president of the United States, inoculated his Continental Army. He understood that the risk of a smallpox epidemic decimating his men was greater than the risks of inoculation.

Vaccination

In the late 1700s, farmers in Gloucestershire, England, noticed that dairymaids always had fair complexions. Most other women's faces were pockmarked from smallpox. Although dairymaids were known to catch a milder disease, called cowpox, from the cows they milked, the scars from cowpox disappeared and the dairymaids never came down with smallpox afterward.

In 1774, a Dorset farmer named Benjamin Jesty decided to inoculate his wife and children with cowpox rather than smallpox. He hoped this would protect them from smallpox—like the dairymaids. Although his family was exposed to smallpox, they never developed the disease. Jesty told Edward Jenner, his country physician, and Jenner decided to test the observation.

Two years after Jesty's experiment, Jenner took the fluid from a cowpox pustule on the wrist of a dairymaid and rubbed it onto the skin of a young boy named James Phipps. Then, even though Jenner tried again and again to give Phipps smallpox, the boy never caught it.

Jenner called this process vaccination, after the French word for cow: *vache*. The country doctor wrote up his research, but it was ignored by the medical establishment in London. Jenner continued experimenting and realized that a big selling point for vaccination was that it carried no risk for spreading smallpox.

English physicians were suspicious and slow to accept vaccination. It took another hundred years for scientists to figure out why inoculation and vaccination worked—and another half century after that to isolate the smallpox virus particle under an electron microscope. Jenner did, however, eventually receive honors and a cash prize for his discovery. And the hide of Blossom the cow, from whom he took material for his experiments, is still on display in a London hospital library.

Extinction

In 1979, the World Health Organization announced that smallpox had been eradicated after a ten-year program that vaccinated all the people in every country where the disease was reported, no matter how remote. Somalia was the last country to report a victim of the disease.

Return to Sender: Syphilis and Scurvy

Europeans carried their diseases to the New World, but what did they get in return? Syphilis is a disease that swept across Europe just after the first conquistadors returned from the Americas, and scurvy haunted the lives of explorers on the sailing ships that followed.

Syphilis

Syphilis, a sexually transmitted bacterial disease, is usually blamed on someone else. The Italians called it the Spanish disease, the English called it the French disease, the French called it the Italian disease, the Russians called it the Polish disease, the Arabs called it the Christian disease, and in India it was known as the foreigner's disease. Maybe the Chinese had it right—they called it the pleasure disease.

The symptoms of syphilis can be horrific. The first small pellet-like sore emerges three weeks after infection. It appears where the bacterium entered the body, typically on the genitals. The sore may go unnoticed.

The disease disappears for a number of weeks, but then it returns, causing the patient to have an overall sick feeling—sore throat, swollen glands, headache, and tiredness. Sufferers also experience patchy hair loss and a non-itchy rash on the palms of the hands and soles of the feet. Then the disease disappears again and may not come back for years or even decades.

In its final stage, abscesses eat away the nose, lips, bones, and genitals. Sufferers can go blind, lose their coordination, become paralyzed, or experience dementia before they die. Mothers can pass on the disease to their unborn children. Today, thankfully, we can treat the disease with antibiotics.

There are different theories to explain how syphilis spread to the Old World. In one story, which takes place in 1493, Charles VIII of France marched an army down the Italian peninsula to claim the Kingdom of Naples. He hired Spanish soldiers, fresh from Columbus's voyage, to enlarge his force. These Spaniards socialized with local women and passed on syphilis, which they'd contracted in the New World. The disease spread quickly and savagely because the Europeans carried no resistance.

Eventually, Charles had to retreat—and he died of syphilis in 1498.

Other scientists now think that the disease probably didn't come from the New World. Late-stage syphilis leaves scars on the skull, but no such telltale signs have been confirmed on New World skeletons. As well, in a monastery in England, syphilis scars have been found on skulls that date seventy years before Columbus's voyage. Hmmm—now we're blaming the English ...

Syphilis probably mutated into a sexually transmitted disease from a milder related disease called yaws, which afflicted ancestral humans. It's likely that all the moving around that happened during Columbus's explorations and Charles's war spread this new Old World disease.

Scurvy

When Columbus returned from the Americas with his stories of exploration, healthy young men from all over Europe signed up to serve their countries in discovering or protecting newly claimed lands. Many of these sailors dreamed of adventure, the wonders of the world, and the possibility of riches. They understood the risks of enduring storms in a wooden sailing ship, getting lost, and shipwreck, but they looked forward to the challenge of facing the elements using their wits and muscles in a team effort. Fun!

After a few months at sea, some sailors found that—instead of getting stronger with the exercise and experience—their muscles weakened and they lost the will to work. They crawled into their hammocks to rest and even die.

Scurvy creeps over its victims slowly. Its first symptoms include gloominess, listlessness, and physical exhaustion. Sufferers lose coordination, their skin bruises easily, their joints ache, and their hands and feet swell.

After a month or more, their gums become spongy and bleed, and their teeth fall out—and so do their nails and hair. Skin turns yellowish and rubbery. Bleeding under the skin leaves purple blotches. Healed broken bones separate again. Old scars gape open and bleed. In the late stages of the disease, the simple action of sitting up quickly can rupture an internal organ and cause the victim to bleed to death.

The sleeping quarters below deck on these sailing ships filled up with the sick—it looked like an epidemic. But scurvy is not an infectious disease. It's a nutritional deficiency of vitamin C—a fact that no one understood at the time. Without vitamin C, or ascorbic acid, our bodies cannot make the protein collagen, which binds and connects our tissues and bones together.

We get vitamin C mostly from certain fresh foods, with high doses in fruits such as lemons, oranges, and limes, and in vegetables such as spinach, broccoli, and parsley. A standard ship's diet of biscuit, cooked and salted meat or fish, and beer contained zero vitamin C.

Portuguese explorers and privateers knew that drinking a few swigs of lemon juice every day kept scurvy away as early as 1397—but that practice disappeared by the early 1600s. The idea of preventing a disease that had not yet erupted made no sense to sea captains—especially if they had to pay for expensive lemon juice.

Meanwhile, European doctors looked for cures using the classical theory of the humors—imbalances in the body's yellow bile, black bile, phlegm, and blood. Scurvy could be balanced, some thought, by spooning vinegar into the mouth. Others recommended a strong laxative to empty the bowels or a poisonous patent medicine called Ward's Pill and Drop which caused violent sweating, vomiting, and diarrhea. Over the next two hundred years, tens of thousands of sailors died of scurvy.

In 1747, a young English ship's surgeon named James Lind sailed on the HMS *Salisbury*, a ship cruising the English Channel, looking for invading Spanish warships. It wasn't long before eighty of the crew fell seriously ill with scurvy. Lind persuaded the captain to allow him to run an experiment to see which of six supposed treatments could cure scurvy. Surprisingly, the captain agreed—but the sailors did not. No matter! Lind hung the hammocks of twelve of the sickest sailors together in a separate hold and fed them all the same kinds and amounts of food—gruel, broth, biscuit, barley, rice, dried currants, raisins, and wine.

The men continued to be very sick while eating this diet. He then divided the men into pairs and added one "cure"—cider; vinegar; elixir of vitriol; sea water; two oranges and a lemon; or a medicinal paste of garlic, mustard, and tamarind—to the diets of each pair. After two weeks, the two men who had eaten the oranges and lemon were up and helping tend the sick. The two on cider rations felt better but were still too weak to work. All the other sailors had become sicker.

Despite Lind's results, only a few ships' captains followed his recommendations. Those who prescribed citrus defeated scurvy on board—including Captain James Cook during his voyages of discovery in the Pacific Ocean—and those who did not often lost more men due to scurvy than any other cause, including battle. But the obvious statistics were ignored.

In 1793, Sir Gilbert Blane, a physician but also an aristocrat, advised his friend, an admiral on the warship HMS *Suffolk*, to give a daily dose of lemon juice to all the sailors on their voyage to the East Indies. After more than twenty-three weeks at sea, scurvy claimed no lives. Using this example as well as statistics that compared death by scurvy to death by enemy action, Blane persuaded the British Navy to adopt citrus rations for all sailors—earning them the nickname "limeys."

It is interesting to note that Native Canadians had a cure, too. When French settlers came to Canada and stayed through winter, they had no fresh fruits and vegetables to eat and suffered from scurvy. The Native Canadians shared their remedy—tea made from fresh spruce needles. Spruce needles are richer in vitamin C than lemon juice! Those who drank the tea got better.

The Black Vomit aka Yellow Fever

In 1793, when Stubbins Ffirth was nine years old, yellow fever killed five thousand people in Philadelphia, Pennsylvania. Nine years later, as a young medical student at the University of Pennsylvania, Ffirth set out to demonstrate that yellow fever is not contagious. He'd noticed that caregivers of the sick did not necessarily get sick themselves and reasoned that yellow fever spread in another way.

A unique and startling symptom of yellow fever is black vomit. So Ffirth chose to sleep in bed sheets covered in the black vomit of a yellow fever victim. He did not get the disease. Next, he cut his arms and rubbed black vomit into the wounds. He did not get yellow fever. He dropped black vomit into his eyes—no reaction. Then he heated up some vomit and inhaled the fumes. When that didn't make him sick, he ate the black vomit. Still healthy, he covered himself in the blood, saliva, and urine of yellow fever victims, and when he continued to remain well, he felt he'd proven the disease is not contagious. There was one big problem, though—people didn't believe his story (or that his name had two *f*'s in it).

But Ffirth was right. We now know that humans catch yellow fever from the bite of an infected mosquito, *Aedes aegypti*, and not from contact with other people.

Yellow fever attacks a victim's liver, causing jaundice, which turns the skin yellow. Sufferers experience very high fever, headache, back and leg pain, and terrible vomiting. The vomit is black because victims bleed into their stomach, where the blood darkens. For a long time, people called this disease the black vomit.

Yellow fever probably originated in Africa and crossed the Atlantic to the New World on slave ships. When smallpox and other Old World diseases killed off so many Native Americans, ruthless coffee and sugar plantation owners brought in Africans to do their backbreaking labor—free slave labor, at that.

The mosquito that spreads the yellow fever virus can survive on sailing ships by laying its eggs in water casks. The insect can thrive for several generations at sea, picking up the virus from the blood of sick passengers and passing it on to new victims on board. Finally, both mosquitoes and sick passengers disembark and infest new populations.

Mosquitoes die off in winter in cold territories—like the Northern United States and Canada—but they thrive year-round in warm climates.

In the New World, terrible outbreaks occurred in Jamaica, Cuba, Haiti, and ports up the Eastern Seaboard as far as Quebec. Native Americans, Europeans, and Asians died in large numbers in these places. Africans who had just disembarked from the slave ships seemed to be more resistant, and so—in a cruel twist—the slave trade increased. When the slaves in Haiti rebelled against French plantation owners in 1802, Napoléon Bonaparte's army was unable to win the island back because so many of his troops died of yellow fever.

The next year, the French sold Louisiana to the United States because a huge number of their colonists in New Orleans had died from yellow fever. An attempt by the French to dig the Panama Canal had to be abandoned in 1893 after twenty-two thousand workers died. In order to protect their workers from insects, the French had tried placing the legs of their beds in water—only to provide a perfect egg-laying habitat for mosquitoes and increase the death count!

When yellow fever first appeared on the Eastern Seaboard, people blamed sick oysters, the smell of dead fish, thunderstorms, earthquakes, godless living—you name it! They tried spreading quicklime or coal dust in the streets and igniting bonfires to prevent it. They thought bloodletting, dunking in ice water, or drinking lemonade might cure it.

Some noticed that yellow fever clustered around ships and dockyards—but that it didn't seem to travel inland. Others started to acknowledge, like Ffirth, that the people who took care of the sick didn't always get sick themselves, realizing that yellow fever wasn't contagious.

About eighty years after Ffirth's experiments, Carlos Finlay, a Cuban-born doctor, proposed that mosquitoes transmitted yellow fever. He conducted 104 experiments in which volunteers were exposed to mosquitoes that had bitten yellow fever victims—but none of his volunteers got sick.

When Dr. Walter Reed, an American army major and physician, joined Finlay in Cuba in 1900, he tried another experiment. Reed lengthened the amount of time between when the mosquito was exposed to the disease and when it was released on the volunteer—and he found that those volunteers did get sick. His work was called "silly" in newspaper editorials back in the United States.

Reed contrived another experiment to prove this theory. He set up volunteers in three screened areas. In one, volunteers slept in the soiled pyjamas of yellow fever victims on black vomit–covered bedding. Into the second, he released mosquitoes that had recently bitten yellow fever victims. In the third enclosed area, volunteers remained without mosquitoes or soiled pajamas.

Only the volunteers exposed to mosquitoes got yellow fever. The volunteers who slept in smeared pajamas on black vomit–covered beds were held there for sixty-three days— and they still didn't get sick!

Although Reed did not produce a cure for yellow fever, he showed that by controlling mosquitoes he could protect people from getting the disease. His findings enabled the Americans to complete the construction of the Panama Canal in 1914 with no deaths caused by yellow fever.

Max Theiler, a South African virologist working in New York, finally perfected a vaccine for yellow fever. He won the Nobel Prize for medicine in 1951 for his work.

One question—why did Ffirth not contract yellow fever when he cut his arms and rubbed black vomit into the open wounds? His actions were similar to a mosquito injecting virus into the bloodstream with her bite. Scientists think that the vomit of dying yellow fever patients does not contain a lot of active virus—Ffirth was just lucky!

Superstition to Science

In 1634, King Charles I of England suspected that a certain old woman who practiced the healing arts was, in fact, a witch. He ordered Dr. William Harvey, his personal physician, to investigate.

The doctor traveled by carriage to her hovel. At first, the old woman wouldn't let Harvey in, but he cajoled her, explaining that he was a wizard and wanted to meet her familiar, *a supernatural being that acts as a witch's helper. Harvey assumed that her familiar would be a cat. Impressed by the doctor's charm and courtly wig, she opened her door and directed him to a cupboard—and out hopped a toad. The old woman offered her toad a saucer of cream.*

Harvey gave the woman a coin and asked her to walk to a local inn to bring him back some beer. When she left the hovel, Harvey grabbed the toad and cut it open. He examined its heart, lungs, and intestines. He decided it was not supernatural, just a common toad.

When the woman returned with the beer, she saw that he'd killed her toad. She shrieked, hit him hard, pulled his wig, and scratched his face. Harvey escaped to his carriage covered in cuts and bruises.

Dr. Harvey was no ordinary physician. Years before his dissection of the toad, he wrote about the function of the heart and circulation of blood in humans. His work contradicted the theories of the fathers of medicine— especially Galen of Pergamon—and was dismissed by many of his colleagues. However, the king supported him, and so—eventually— did future generations. A man of science, Harvey still had to cut open a toad to prove that it wasn't supernatural. He lived in a time when the medical world see-sawed between *belief in tradition, even superstition, and belief in scientifically tested observation.*

In the Age of Discovery, Europeans celebrated the finding of new lands and peoples but were slow to accept fresh ideas or discoveries in medicine. Most doctors were not like Harvey. They clung to the traditional theory of the humors. Other folk on the fringes of the medical world, like the old woman, based their practices on superstition. But medicine founded on scientific evidence did take a few steps forward in these years—including the acceptance of vaccination for smallpox and the citrus supplement for scurvy. Some new theories were developed too—and survived the test of time either in alternative or mainstream medicine.

One was the theory of plant signatures. Patterns in nature fascinated Jakob Böhme in the seventeenth century. He suggested that plant parts that resemble body parts could be used to treat complaints. For example, the liver-shaped leaves of mayflowers would help treat liver diseases. Walnuts, which look like brain matter, could cure headaches. These theories excited the medical community for a while and continue to interest herbalists today.

In the eighteenth century, Samuel Hahnemann proposed a theory of similarities. He said that "like" would cure "like." So an onion that causes a runny nose cures the common cold. Hahnemann's theories and medicines developed into present-day homeopathy.

In the sixteenth century, Girolamo Fracastoro of Verona suggested that disease had nothing to do with humors. He proposed that disease entered the body as seeds. These seeds then multiplied and caused illness. This led him to note that different diseases had different seeds—an early theory of germs. He recommended personal and public hygiene to prevent disease. Fracastoro's ideas were generally ignored until, in 1675, Antony van Leeuwenhoek created a microscope lens powerful enough to actually see some of these seeds, or germs. Real evidence proved this theory—and today Fracastoro's ideas are part of mainstream, science-based medicine.

Little by little, doctors began to look at contagions in new ways. We can track the slow modern understanding of contagious disease by looking at when people started using existing common words to describe medical issues:

Epidemic, circa 400 BC

Contagious, 1350 AD

Virus, 1728 AD

Vaccination, 1796 AD

Germ, 1802 AD

Protozoa, 1818 AD

Bacteria, 1840 AD

Microbe, 1868 AD

Immunity, 1879 AD

THE INDUSTRIAL AGE (1800–1900): PROSPERITY, POLLUTION, and PANDEMICS

Cholera: Death by Drinking Water

"The Cholera Treatment Unit is working smoothly. It has seen about 150 patients since the epidemic began; five of those people have died. We step in chlorine shoe baths on our way into the Unit and have our hands washed with a high chlorine solution and soap. The doctor is Haitian, trained in Cuba. He talks about the speed with which cholera attacks, how it can quickly dehydrate you. In the recovery room, he introduces me to a patient who is ready to leave. 'Two days ago she was admitted. She was crying, but she was so dehydrated she couldn't make any tears. Now she's ready to go home. We know how to beat this disease.'"

Diary entry by David Morley,
CEO, Save the Children
January 4, 2011, Gaston Magron
Health Services, Haiti

The cholera bacterium—*Vibrio cholerae*, named for its wiggling motion—occurs naturally where disaster and poverty collide. It crashes ashore on the waves of tsunamis, does the rounds of refugee camps and slums, and, as in the case in Haiti, thrives on the chaos following an earthquake.

Victims contract cholera by drinking water or eating food that is fouled by the excrement of other cholera sufferers. Once inside the body, cholera moves rapidly. Patients can lose so much liquid through diarrhea that they can die within two hours. Crippled by cramps, untreated patients waste away as their intestinal linings slough off as fishy-smelling stools that look like dirty dishwater. Dehydration and loss of salt result in falling blood pressure, a racing heart,

70

the breaking of tiny blood vessels called capillaries, hollow eyes, and skin that's blue and wrinkled. In their misery, victims curl up and die, often in the fetal position.

Cholera lives naturally in the environment today and probably originated in the Bay of Bengal, India. Although thought to have been around since ancient times, cholera gathered pandemic strength once people left farms for towns and cities. Poor sanitation and overcrowding in Indian cities, such as Calcutta, brought about the first major outbreak in 1817. The pandemic began when cholera bacteria, living in copepods (crustaceans) in the Bay of Bengal, came ashore in a storm and contaminated the local drinking water. Over the next few years, about fifteen million Indians died.

How does a bacterium go viral? Ships take in controlled amounts of water called ballast to maintain stability at sea. When ships sucked up ballast from the Bay of Bengal, the water they took on board was teeming with cholera bacteria from the untreated sewage of cholera patients. The ballast helped the ships sail on an even keel while traveling, but when water was removed from the ballast tanks and dumped in the bay in another port, cholera let loose a new storm of disease. There have been seven more global pandemics since then, as ships and travelers spread the disease across the Middle East, into Europe, and beyond.

Every year, between three and five million people fall sick with cholera, and over one hundred thousand die worldwide. Nearly four thousand people died following the earthquake in Haiti.

Cholera is a preventable disease. There is an effective cholera vaccine to stop the disease before it starts. For those who do become infected, IV fluids and antibiotics can quicken recovery. Oral rehydration drinks are a cheap and satisfactory cure, bringing eight out of ten patients back from the brink in just a few days.

In an emergency situation, all that's needed is sterile water, sugar, and salt. But in a place ripped apart by war or natural disaster, even these simple ingredients can be hard to find, and many people can't afford bottled rehydration drinks. Cholera is almost never reported in the developed world, but it is on the rise in the world's poorest countries such as Haiti, Dominican Republic, Uganda, and Zimbabwe.

Portrait of an Epidemiologist

John Snow (1813–1858), the world's first epidemiologist, was an English physician who was also curious about the spread of disease. He studied London's 1854 outbreak of cholera, tracking down and recording deaths on a map.

At the time, unregulated private companies supplied citizens with water, and people bought their water from specific pumps. His detective work showed that most cases of cholera came from within a short distance of one shallow well that was dug near a cesspool. The Broad Street pump brought the water to the surface. He interviewed the families of victims living farther away and found that they also bought their water from the Broad Street pump—because they preferred its taste. Snow looked at water samples from the well under a microscope and saw "white, flocculent particles" that he connected with cholera.

Snow himself tended many cholera patients but never got sick. It made sense to him that cholera was carried into the body by drinking water and not by breathing bad air or miasma. He presented his findings and showed his map—known as The Ghost Map—to the London authorities. At his urging, the pump handle was removed and the outbreak stopped.

Preventative medicine at work! Or, so you'd think. Unfortunately, Snow's conclusions were not taken seriously. As soon as the threat of cholera was gone, a new pump handle was installed. People didn't want to believe that they were drinking water laced with neighborhood sewage. It took at least twenty more years for people to understand that miasmas don't spread cholera. But Snow's principal findings ring true today: safe drinking water and proper sewage treatment can eliminate this scourge forever.

Ignaz Semmelweis and Florence Nightingale—Connecting Health and Cleanliness

Ignaz Semmelweis

You would never plunge your hands into a rotting carcass, pluck around with your bare fingers, roughly wipe your hands on a cloth, and then touch an open cut on a friend's leg. Why not? For starters, you'd wear gloves and a mask and thoroughly wash between handling something putrid and touching a living person. So why did doctors in the early to mid-1800s dissect corpses in one room and deliver babies in the next without a bar of soap between them?

Back then, the medical profession was in its infancy, and patient care was primitive. Understanding and accepting the causes of most common diseases were still in the future. Despite limited tools and drugs, doctors pledged to do the best they could. Most trained as apprentices in hospitals and with individual physicians, learning the beliefs and techniques of their teachers and rarely challenging their elders. Occasionally, a young doctor who looked at the bigger picture would come along, identifying obvious problems and speaking out.

Ignaz Semmelweis was one of those doctors. Specializing in obstetrics in the 1840s, he worked with two maternity wards at a hospital in Vienna, Austria. In one ward, doctors and medical students attended pregnant women, in the other, midwives and their apprentices. The doctors moved back and forth between the morgue and the maternity ward, while the midwives stayed with the living patients. Childbed fever, a fever caused by an infection (sepsis) after childbirth, killed 29 percent of medical ward patients but only 3 percent of patients on the midwifery ward. Semmelweis did the math, but his colleagues refused to believe that they could make their patients ill.

In 1847, one of the senior doctors, Professor Jakob Kolletschka, cut his finger while performing an autopsy and developed an infection identical to that of the women on the maternity ward. When Kolletschka died, Semmelweis connected the dots and insisted on hand-washing with chlorinated water before every delivery. Childbed fever almost disappeared overnight. You'd think that Semmelweis would have been hailed as a hero for his discovery, but the opposite actually occurred.

Frustrated by the stupidity of his colleagues, he left Vienna and returned to his native Budapest, Hungary. Again, Semmelweis introduced hand-washing and the number of deaths from childbed fever fell to near zero. His Hungarian colleagues challenged his reasoning, and Semmelweis finally went mad. He was admitted to hospital and died a few weeks later of sepsis—the same infection he had worked to eliminate.

Florence Nightingale

Semmelweis may have been a forward thinker, but Florence Nightingale, the founder of modern nursing, was *way* ahead of her time.

Born into a wealthy English family in 1820, Nightingale's future should have been predictable: a genteel education in music, embroidery, and perhaps French; a spoiled youth with dances and holidays by the sea; suitable marriage, lots of servants, children, and a life of leisure. Her family did not approve, but she veered off this path and blazed her own. She studied mathematics, traveled to Europe, and volunteered at hospitals and orphanages—all the while keeping notes and records of her experiences.

Nightingale believed in the miasma theory of infection—foul air was responsible for disease—but she was also a stickler for cleanliness. As superintendent of London's Institution for the Care of Sick Gentlewomen in Distressed Circumstances in 1853, Nightingale observed that patients and their beds were dirty, that water was scarce, and that nutrition was poor.

She demanded things change. Starting with the basics, she ordered healthy meals, proper plumbing, clean laundry, clean bandages, and ventilation. She didn't know that her high standards of hygiene would reduce infection and speed healing.

Florence Nightingale earned the name Lady of the Lamp when she applied her methods of cleanliness to field hospitals during the Crimean War of 1854. She worked tirelessly by day, but she also checked on wounded soldiers by lamplight at night, establishing around-the-clock nursing care.

For Nightingale, neglect was not an option. Before her regime of mops, soap, and clean sheets, almost half of the wounded died. After, the death rate fell to 2 percent. Like Semmelweis, she met resistance within the medical profession as well as from the military, but when the war was over, her work earned respect and honor back home in England.

Nightingale's long-lasting contribution was the establishment of the world's first professional nursing school in London's St. Thomas' Hospital in 1860. To this day,

graduating nurses take the Nightingale Pledge and celebrate International Nurses Day every year on her birthday, May 12.

Tuberculosis: What's Romantic about Coughing and Spitting?

Elizabeth knew something was very wrong before she even opened the door. Dad's car was in the driveway at four o'clock on a Tuesday. Her fears deepened when she saw her parents sitting in the living room, looking sad. Had someone died?

Elizabeth's mother explained that Dad was going to a sanatorium, a hospital exclusively for patients with tuberculosis, or TB. He would be isolated for about a year with other TB patients, breathe fresh air, eat nutritious food, and receive vigorous and extensive antibiotic therapy. Incredibly, the year was 1963. Dad wasn't a soldier going off to war or a convicted criminal confined to prison, but he was going away just the same.

Dad caught TB from a coworker who'd recently moved from Eastern Europe. The man had been infected with TB as a child, and the disease had been dormant for years. Recently, it had quietly reactivated, making him infectious. Before he'd known he was sick, he'd passed the disease on to Elizabeth's dad.

Children younger than twelve couldn't visit, but every Sunday for the next sixteen months, Elizabeth sat in the car in the parking lot of the sanatorium and waited for Dad's wave from the window. After he was discharged, doctors said he was cured, but he would always test TB-positive and a chest X-ray would show the scars on his healed lungs. Despite making a full recovery, doctors knew that his TB could reactivate in the future.

Fifty years ago, tuberculosis was uncommon in North America and the developed world. An accurate skin test that identified those patients with the disease—even those without symptoms—and antibiotics to fight the infection had nearly wiped out this dreaded illness. What was it like before antibiotics? That's a very different story!

Tuberculosis, TB, consumption, white plague, wasting disease—whatever you call it, the course is predictable. Patients who develop active TB and are not treated suffer a slow, downhill course of health and usually die. In one form of the illness, patients' symptoms progress very quickly, and this is called galloping consumption.

Pulmonary tuberculosis, the most common form of tuberculosis, settles in the lungs and creeps up on the victim like a mild cold. But once a cough begins, the tuberculosis bacterium digs into the lung tissue. When the patient starts hacking up blood followed by gobs of mucus mixed with particles of tissue, TB has obviously taken hold.

Fever, chest pains, night sweats, and chills further drain energy from the body. Eating becomes difficult and body weight drops drastically. Nearing death, the patient looks like a skeleton on the outside, with lungs resembling foul cottage cheese on the inside.

People domesticated cattle and began drinking unpasteurized milk (now a known way to get TB) between six and eight thousand years ago. And ancient human remains, including the mummy of King Tut, show evidence of tuberculosis. Today, TB still causes up to three million deaths a year worldwide. TB has been labeled the number one cause of death of all time.

Before modern treatment, people tried a variety of desperate so-called cures: eating lobster, drinking donkey's milk, taking a long sea voyage, breathing the smoke from burning cow plops, and eating mice boiled in oil. Surgeons also tried their hand at finding a cure, but these radical procedures—including the deliberate collapsing of the lung to allow it to rest, and the removal of ribs—proved useless.

Great medical minds puzzled over the mysteries of tuberculosis, with observations and theories

adding to our understanding over time. Hippocrates, the ancient Greek physician, called the disease *phthisis*, meaning "to waste." He came close to understanding the source of infection by connecting phthisis with air.

Aristotle, the Greek genius who lived from 384 to 322 BC, correctly suggested that phthisis could be spread from one person to another.

It wasn't until 1650 AD in Germany that anatomist Franciscus Sylvius discovered that the lungs of those dying of TB were full of little nodules he called tubercles.

In 1865, the French physician Jean Antoine Villemin scientifically proved that TB was infectious and not hereditary. During his laboratory experiments, he passed the illness from both people and cattle onto rabbits. Despite the fact that about one in four of all people died of TB, most of Villemin's fellow scientists ignored his results and refused to isolate TB patients from the general public. In Poland, however, at about this time, the first tuberculosis sanatorium hospital opened.

While giving a lecture on March 24, 1882, Robert Koch, a German bacteriologist, rocked the scientific community when he revealed he'd isolated the bacterium responsible for tuberculosis. From the podium, he railed, "If the importance of a disease for mankind is measured by the number of fatalities it causes, then tuberculosis must be considered much more important than those most feared infectious diseases, plague, cholera, and the like."

Then he invited the astonished audience to look at his specimen slides under the microscope. He didn't want his colleagues to dismiss his words, so he brought the slides as physical proof they could see with their own eyes.

Koch tried to develop a vaccine for tuberculosis, but he didn't succeed. When he cultured and sterilized tubercle bacterium and injected it into a patient, it did not prevent TB. However, his work did form the basis for a valuable diagnostic tool—the TB skin test. Still used today, this test identifies if a patient has been exposed to TB. One in four people in the world today produce a positive TB skin test.

Koch's work inspired city governments to improve sanitation. New York led the way by banning public spitting in 1896, hoping to reduce the spread of tuberculosis. The bacterium can also survive in the moist droplets expelled through sneezing, coughing, singing, laughing, and talking.

Koch was awarded the Nobel Prize in 1905 for his contribution to the tuberculosis puzzle, but a cure was still years away. It took almost four decades to piece it all together.

In 1944, Americans Selman Waksman and his graduate student Albert Schatz discovered an antibiotic—streptomycin—that kills the tubercle bacterium.

But tuberculosis, like a rat, is a super-survivor. In a few short years, the bacterium mutated or changed, and streptomycin could no longer do the job alone. Soon, a cocktail of several antibiotics was needed—taken for six months or longer. Still, TB was in retreat, the number of cases fell, and the once-full sanatoriums closed for lack of patients.

The modern medicine community thought they'd conquered the enemy, and Western governments cancelled TB control programs. Then, in the late 1980s, tuberculosis came back, attacking vulnerable members of society: those who were HIV-positive, intravenous drug users, and people living in confined areas such as prisons, nursing homes, crowded urban neighborhoods, and in large, extended family groups on First Nations reserves.

In Nunavut, the largest territory in Canada, the infection rate is sixty-two times higher than in southern Canada. Some municipalities offer incentives such as a free hamburger and fries to patients who stick with the long course of antibiotics. In Canada, governments publish an educational comic book that teaches readers that TB is curable.

Families such as Elizabeth's remember the pain of tuberculosis—physical discomfort combined with separation from loved ones. Back when TB loomed over society and everyone knew someone with the disease, folklore connected TB with a creative mind. In the nineteenth and twentieth centuries, many celebrities died of TB—such as musician Frédéric Chopin, poet John Keats, former First Lady of the United States Eleanor Roosevelt, and screen actress Vivien Leigh. The ghastly symptoms of tuberculosis were made romantic in books, operas, and movies. Heroines were thin, rosy cheeked, and glassy-eyed. "Coughing blood into a silk handkerchief, she took her last breath, blowing a kiss to her beloved."

The Legacy of Louis Pasteur: From His Laboratory to the Sickbed

Madeleine lay pale and listless on bedsheets soaked from her feverish sweat. Wiping off the mustard plaster poultice with a warm towel, Maman shook her head as Madeleine coughed again. She was definitely worse. Finally, her worried parents agreed they'd better send for the doctor.

Claude, her elder brother, ran to the stable, saddled his pony, and sped off down the dirt track into the last light of day. When the doctor arrived the next morning with his horse and buggy, he came in through the tradesmen's entrance, hanging his coat in the back kitchen.

Madeleine's breathing was shallow as he opened his doctor's bag and laid out its contents on the bedspread: two bottles of tonic, one elixir for cough, a packet of dried herbs, tweezers, a leather pouch protecting a scalpel, and a vial of squirming leeches. Lastly, he pulled out a shiny new stethoscope—an instrument the family had never seen before.

In the mid-1800s, people throughout the world dreaded sickness. About half of all European babies died before they turned two. If a male survived until his fiftieth birthday, he was lucky.

Females usually died younger, often in childbirth.

When patients such as Madeleine spiked a fever, they were sponged with cool water and given herbal tea to drink. Infected tonsils were removed with a primitive surgical instrument called a tonsil guillotine, and the surgeon didn't wash his hands or sterilize his tools.

Bloodletting was a cure-all for the sick and a preventative measure for the healthy. With limited knowledge and resources, the medical profession knew so little—yet they had no idea how little they knew!

Today, that has all changed thanks in large part to the groundwork of Louis Pasteur.

On December 27, 1822, Louis Pasteur was born into a family of tanners. Tanning is a process that uses chemicals to transform animal skins (which naturally rot and stink) into leather that endures for years as saddles, chairs, boots, and so on. His hardworking family schooled Pasteur in the importance of following the steps of a recipe, and this proved to be an excellent set of skills for a future chemist.

Later in life, as a professor in chemistry, Pasteur compared his laboratory experiments to detective work. Beginning with a mystery, he gradually peeled away layers, eventually solving a problem. His persnickety scientific methods raised the bar for other scientists—and brought him admirers as well as rivals. He believed that "chance favors only the prepared mind"—lucky discoveries are made by alert and ready thinkers. As head of the department of chemistry in 1854 at University of Strasbourg, in France, Pasteur figured out the process of fermentation. Fermentation is a chemical reaction that turns decomposing grain or fruit into alcohol. His discovery made it possible for beer and wine to be produced on a large scale.

Pasteur also helped a manufacturer determine why his beet juice vinegar went sour. On this case, he looked at the vinegar under a microscope and observed tiny microbes. He heated the beet juice and killed the microbes, making the juice sterile. This process, later named pasteurization, revolutionized food safety.

What does pasteurization have to do with health or pandemics? The pasteurization of milk greatly reduced the incidence of tuberculosis and salmonella poisoning from eating rotten milk or cheese.

Pasteur refused to believe in spontaneous generation—a theory that had been accepted since the Middle Ages and was supported by Bible stories—which describes the creation of living things from non-living matter.

A popular proof dating back to the mid-1600s supporting spontaneous generation was the sudden appearance of mice in a pail of grain where soiled, sweaty underwear had been left for twenty-one days. A keen observer would soon discover that mice came to feed on the grain, and the underwear provided comfy bedding.

An experiment conducted by an Englishman named John Needham in 1745 provided another example to support spontaneous generation. He boiled chicken broth, killing all microbes. Then he allowed the broth to sit, uncovered, at room temperature. When it became cloudy, he reasoned new life had "sprung forth" from the broth—evidence of spontaneous generation.

Pasteur disproved Needham's claim by repeating the experiment, but this time, Pasteur stored the broth in a swan-neck flask, preventing microbes from reaching the sterile broth.

As an alternative to spontaneous

generation, Pasteur proposed his "germ theory." He insisted that microbes, or germs, were the scientific cause for the spark that triggers disease. He set about isolating the microbes responsible for deathly diseases such as anthrax and rabies, with the hope of preventing the spread of these infections.

Edward Jenner, from England, created the first vaccine in 1774, but he never knew why it worked. Pasteur solved the riddle of vaccination and tried applying the idea to other microbes.

Pasteur's German rival, Robert Koch, isolated the anthrax bacterium that lives in soil and kills livestock. Pasteur used Koch's bacterium to develop a vaccine and he tested it on cattle, sheep, and a goat. He conducted his experiment in public so that everyone could see his methods, making it difficult for naysayers to criticize the results. All the animals he vaccinated and then exposed to an anthrax culture survived. Those exposed to just the disease died. The success of this experiment gave Pasteur more evidence for his germ theory.

Rabies was a harder case to crack. Until this point in time, rabies had always been fatal. Even though Pasteur knew it was a virus, he could not see it with his ordinary microscope. Through experiments on rabbits and then dogs,

Pasteur learned that rabies has a long incubation period. It eventually became clear that rabies could not be prevented, but Pasteur hoped a vaccine might be a cure.

He devised a series of fourteen vaccines that increased in strength, and gave infected animals one injection per day for two weeks. The dogs that he'd vaccinated lived; the others died of rabies.

Joseph Meister, a nine-year-old boy who'd been bitten fifteen times by a rabid dog two days earlier, was Pasteur's first human test subject. It was July 1885. When Joseph's doctor couldn't help him, the doctor suggested his family try Pasteur, even though Pasteur lacked medical qualifications.

The boy received the same fourteen-day regime as Pasteur's dogs—and lived. Today, domestic pets are vaccinated to prevent rabies, and people who are bitten still receive a series of painful needles to prevent the disease from developing.

Louis Pasteur's legacy continues on in the Institut Pasteur in Paris. Founded in 1887 as a laboratory where Pasteur and his associates worked on infectious diseases and vaccines, it remains an international hub of medical and scientific research.

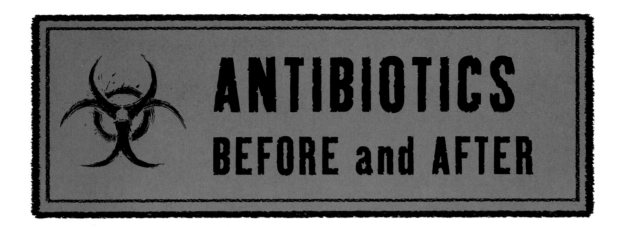

ANTIBIOTICS BEFORE and AFTER

World War I and the Spanish Flu

Coroner's Report
December 5, 1918
This twenty-two-year-old white male was in excellent health before falling ill.

Clinical History
Circumstances leading to death of patient

- Returned with troops from the Great War on steamer ship after the Armistice celebration in France, arriving home November 28, 1918. Admitted to military infirmary on November 30, complaining of mild flu symptoms: head and body aches, sore throat, dizziness, poor appetite, and fever of 39.7°C (103.5°F).
- Patient transferred to hospital. Symptoms developed: drowsy, lethargic, and with low pulse. Bed rest and fluids prescribed by attending doctors. Patient developed a dry cough, but perked up briefly when his temperature returned to normal.
- Sudden relapse on December 2. Fever spiked to 40°C (104°F). Increased cough with blood in mucus. Breathing raspy and patient frequently choked. Died about 11:00 pm.

General Findings
Observations of the exterior of the body

- Skin, especially on face, cyanosed—purplish blue and blotched.
- Foamy mucus in nose and mouth cavities contained dried blood.
- Frequent sneezing and nose-blowing appear to have caused redness of skin around nose and chapped lips.

Observations inside of the body

- Patient constipated—evidence of dehydration.
- Lungs show signs of advanced pneumonia: pus-filled lobes speckled with burst blood vessels.
- Lungs have the consistency of soft blackberry jam. Normal uptake of oxygen would have been severely impaired.
- Toxemia: bacteria from the lungs overwhelmed the bloodstream with infection.

Conclusions

The patient died from a severe case of influenza—likely Spanish flu—possibly acquiring the viral infection during the end-of-war celebrations or in close quarters on board ship. Cause of death was asphyxia, choking on body fluids coughed up from his lungs. He was highly infectious at the time of death. Those who traveled, roomed, and ate with him in the days before he became sick, as well as those who cared for him during his illness should be advised to watch for flu symptoms.

In the last year of World War I, the worst flu pandemic in history traveled the globe, cutting down more people than were killed in the war itself. Estimates range widely, from twenty-one to sixty million people.

Unlike "normal" seasonal flu, which usually targets the very young and old, the 1918 pandemic also overwhelmed people in their twenties and thirties, the fittest and healthiest. And because soldiers gathered in large groups on military bases and boats, in prisoner-of-war camps, and in the trenches, they were sitting ducks for catching flu.

This flu pandemic was unusual—including the name. Why was it called the Spanish flu? Spain was hit hard by the flu. And the rest of the world heard about it through the Spanish media, hence the name.

Conditions of war—such as rationed food, cold homes due to lack of heating fuel, and a stretched-thin health-care system—also gave this nasty flu virus the advantage. The sheer number of deaths created shortages in coffins, undertakers, and gravediggers.

Spain was a neutral country and therefore didn't hide the impact of the flu and the number of deaths. But the countries engaged in combat lowered a veil of secrecy around the numbers of their sick and dead. Neither side wanted to admit that their soldiers were weakened.

Rumors circulated that this pestilence was actually a German biological weapon. But then the flu

reached Germany, too. In fact, the Spanish flu may have turned the tide in favor of the Allies against the Axis powers. A planned assault on England was cancelled because so many front-line German soldiers lay sick, dying, or dead.

Even if politicians and generals had admitted there was a pandemic, we can't be certain much would have changed. Scientists were unable to find the source of the disease and could not develop an effective vaccine. Because this flu struck in the days before electron microscopes, scientists literally couldn't see what they were up against. This particular influenza virus was so small that twenty thousand viral particles could sit on the head of a pin.

Today, because virologists and microbiologists think another pandemic looms, there is still urgent curiosity about the Spanish flu. Scientists hope that by studying specimens reclaimed from old laboratory slides and exhumed bodies they can determine why the Spanish flu was so deadly. They hope that an understanding of how the Spanish flu behaved will help prepare for, or prevent, the next pandemic flu.

For many years, a cook in a Kansas military camp was thought to be the first confirmed Spanish flu case in 1918. He traveled to Europe on board a ship and took the flu with him. But the work of virologists such as Professor John Oxford of England challenged this theory and suggested the cook got sick at the start of a second wave of Spanish flu on European soil. Oxford found that an identical flu did the rounds at a military base in France in 1916 and concluded the flu of 1918 was so intense because it had mutated and become stronger.

Childhood Diseases

"Step on a crack, break your mother's back. Step on a line, break her spine." In the early 1960s, Penny told her friend Janie (now Jane Drake, one of the authors of this book) that this was true—and Janie believed her. Janie chanted the rhyme and skipped down the sidewalk, aiming for smooth pavement, until she bounded up Penny's steps. A huge sign posted by the Medical Officer of Health hung on the front door:

SCARLET FEVER
These premises are under
The Department of Public Health
QUARANTINE

The window on the top floor creaked open and Penny poked her head out and waved. No one could go in, and she couldn't come out. Penny's sister had scarlet fever and the entire family was trapped inside for a week, even the dog. Janie had lots of questions. Stomping home, she forgot about the cracks and lines. This was no time for superstition.

Scarlet Fever

Fifty years ago, when your grandparents were kids, contagious diseases such as scarlet fever routinely infected whole families, spread like wildfire through neighborhoods, and shut down schools. Kids frequently developed serious health complications or even died.

Before antibiotics, people were frightened by a diagnosis of scarlet fever (an infection from the same bacterium that causes strep throat). Most kids who fell ill with this sickness would feel miserable for several weeks, suffering through a sore throat, pus-covered tonsils, peeling skin, chills, vomiting, aches, and pains. A red, sandpaper-like rash would appear, lingering for two or three weeks as a reminder of the "scarlet" in the name.

Most sufferers would get better. But in some cases, the infection would camp out in the ears, sinuses, or chest, making recovery slow and painful. Some suffered pneumonia, meningitis, or kidney or liver problems—leading to longer illness or death.

For unknown reasons, the scarlet fever bacterium gradually weakened and no longer packed the same punch. These days, outbreaks are rare thanks to antibiotics and alert public health workers, but they still occur.

Measles

MMR is an acronym for a combined vaccine for measles, mumps, and rubella. It has saved millions of lives, reduced unnecessary sickness, and prevented uncountable missed school

days. Anyone under forty-five years old was probably vaccinated as a kid.

Some grownups may have sentimental memories of being home sick with measles—Popsicles, ginger ale, cooling chamomile lotion, one-on-one time with Mom, card games, daytime TV—but it remains a serious global illness with twenty million cases a year.

The World Health Organization (WHO) lists measles in the top five diseases that kill children under five—eighteen died every hour in 2008. But this highly contagious virus is preventable by vaccine.

After an incubation period of over a week, sufferers begin to show obvious signs of sickness. The most distinct symptom is a rash that starts on the head and travels down the body over the next week. Sometimes the rash can appear inside the mouth—small red spots with blue-white centers. These dots are called Koplik's spots, named after Henry Koplik, who was the first to document them in 1896.

Some people who contract measles get horrific complications: dehydrating diarrhea, encephalitis (swelling of the brain), or pneumonia. On rare occasions, a sufferer who recovers is left deaf, blind, or mentally disabled. It's no wonder that WHO, UNICEF, and others are taking the lead in eliminating measles worldwide. In the last ten years, these organizations have immunized millions of kids in Africa and Asia—and the infection rate is plummeting.

But measles can still strike in North America. In fact, the headline "Public Health issues warning about measles exposure in downtown Woodstock store" appeared in a small town newspaper in Ontario, Canada, in October 2010. How could this be possible?

It turns out, a visitor from another country, someone who had never been vaccinated, was infected with the highly contagious virus and walked into a decorating store in Woodstock. The threat of infection remained two hours after the sufferer left.

Anyone who had been in the store during that time could have contracted the illness if they hadn't been vaccinated yet, were never vaccinated, or had been improperly vaccinated. Those people who thought they might have been exposed were warned to watch for the classic measles rash.

Before widespread vaccination, Canada reported about three hundred thousand cases of measles every year, with five thousand treated in hospital and several hundred deaths. Since 1998 in Britain, some parents have refused to vaccinate their children because they have been misinformed about the risks of the process. Now there are several thousand cases in Britain every year. A spokesperson for the Department of Public Health wrote, "Until measles is eliminated from the planet like smallpox was, vaccination will continue to be the most important strategy to protect people against this disease."

Mumps

The middle *M* in MMR stands for mumps. Ann Love, one of the authors of this book, remembers her brother asking at dinner, "What's the matter with your neck?" He used his fork to poke toward her. He was usually a pest, but this time he was right. Her face felt full and she was having trouble swallowing her mashed potatoes.

Mumps was going around Toronto in the spring of 1958, and Ann must have breathed in viral droplets from one of her classmate's laughs, sneezes, or coughs. In fact, whoever gave it to her might not have seemed sick.

But Ann got a bad dose of the illness and soon spiked a high fever, lost her appetite, and the glands at the back of her mouth—responsible for making saliva—swelled and ached. Her brother called her Chippie, short for chipmunk, but she was too sick to care.

If she passed along the sickness to him, his testicles might swell and then he wouldn't think it was funny. Other nasty complications could include convulsions and inflammation of the brain and spinal cord. She hoped he wouldn't get it.

Mumps is no longer a menace of childhood. An effective vaccine was developed and introduced in his country by the American microbiologist Maurice Hilleman, in 1967. Today, kids with up-to-date vaccinations don't get mumps. And that's a good thing, because there is no treatment except ice packs and painkillers!

Rubella

Otherwise known as German measles, rubella (the *R* in MMR) is an illness that is milder than measles, but it can have tragic consequences. Pregnant women exposed to the virus who are not immune (meaning that they've never had the disease and were not vaccinated) can miscarry or give birth to a child with severe disabilities. The infection starts out with cold- or flu-like symptoms and a rash appears a day or two later.

Whooping Cough

Whoop, whoop, gasp, gag! Where's the bucket? Vomit. Whooping cough, or pertussis, also starts out like a cold—runny nose, tickle in the throat, and a low-grade fever. Then the diarrhea starts. Finally, the sufferer endures deep spasms in the chest and a cough so wrenching that the capillaries in the eyes can burst, making the white part bright red. When you've got whooping cough, you're in for six weeks of misery.

Whooping cough gets its name from the sound the patient makes when he or she finally takes a deep breath after a coughing jag. Cough medicine can't touch this bacterial infection. Without antibiotics, whooping cough is contagious for at least two weeks.

Normally, doctors say twenty-four hours on antibiotics stops contagious infection, but with whooping cough, it takes five days. It's no wonder whooping cough can quickly turn into an epidemic. The World Health Organization (WHO) reported that sixteen million people had whooping cough in 2008 and 195,000 children died. When will the last whoop be heard? Not until everyone is vaccinated and whooping cough has no one to infect.

Start with a highly infectious bacteria or virus. Add a rash, fever, headache, and cough—and you could have any number of childhood diseases. Over time, we've learned that prevention is better than cure.

The Impact of Antibiotics

After lunch, I sat at my desk and wondered whether I'd eaten something rotten. Heat flushed my neck and face before cramping pain grabbed my middle. Several times during the ride home, I opened the passenger door and threw up on the road. All I could think about was bed. If only I could curl up in a ball and sleep.

But the pain became more intense— had an alien taken hold in my belly? Finally, my family rushed me to hospital. In the ER, a young doctor palpated my abdomen. Her cool hands pressed down slowly, then she let go quickly. As my flesh bounced back into place, the point of agony focused below and to the right of my bellybutton. Wheeling me to the operating room, the nurse asked the doctor if the appendix had ruptured.

This book might not have been written without antibiotics. Both authors of this book had ruptured appendixes that were surgically removed, followed by antibiotics.

The appendix is a little organ attached to the intestine. Doctors can't agree on its function and many believe it's actually unneeded in the human body.

Regardless of the debate, we do know that when the appendix gets infected and bursts, the belly fills with pus. The pain is excruciating. Without antibiotics, the infection can fester, spread, and kill the patient.

Consider your own childhood illnesses: you've probably taken antibiotics for an infected throat, ear, tooth, or cut. In the days before antibiotics, any of these common complaints could have led to prolonged sickness, gross complications, and death. The antibiotic penicillin is probably the most important drug discovered so far.

Alexander Fleming, the microbiologist who discovered penicillin, wasn't always a science nerd. Born into a large Scottish farming family in 1881, he attended a small village school before moving to London, England, in 1895. He had no burning desire to be a scientist. In fact, after two years of college, no particular area of study grabbed his imagination and he took a job as a shipping clerk.

Bored after four years of work, he used a small inheritance to pay for medical school tuition. One summer in between terms, Fleming took a job in the laboratory of vaccine pioneer Almroth Wright. His experiences there lit a fire under him, turning him on to bacteriology and immunology. Despite graduating as a surgeon, Fleming's fascination with infectious disease pulled him back into the laboratory where he happily spent much of his career hunched over a microscope. A nerd at last!

Fleming spent World War I in frontline battlefield hospitals along with his colleagues from Wright's lab. He saw firsthand the horrific effects of bacterial infections that rotted off the body parts of soldiers wounded in trench warfare. He became convinced that a nontoxic antiseptic could be used as a powerful weapon against infection.

Fleming and his colleagues compared the injuries of soldiers. They observed that wounds washed out with standard antiseptics healed more poorly than raw, fresh wounds left to heal on their own. Fleming's group studied the blood and clear liquids that oozed from fresh wounds and discovered that they contained phagocytes, the white blood cells that gobble bacteria.

Fleming realized that the body's own healing powers—the white blood cells—were neutralized by the antiseptics. He tried, unsuccessfully,

to persuade field hospital doctors to cleanse wounds with a nontoxic salt solution instead.

Fleming didn't think he was extraordinary. He believed that new ideas—and sometimes scientific discoveries—came from following hunches, sticking with a problem, and challenging himself. Back in his London laboratory after the war, Fleming studied all forms of secretions—including mucus, tears, pus, and blood serum. He asked his family and friends to give him their sneezed-into tissues—and other specimens—

for his endless experiments. Fleming discovered that the body produces its own natural antiseptic—an enzyme that breaks down the walls of many bad bacteria. Found in saliva, tears, and other body liquids, Fleming called this antiseptic lysozyme. Fleming's plea to use it, rather than wash it away with strong cleansers, was a step forward in understanding wounds.

Fleming's laboratory was not a neat place. But it's this lack of tidiness that led to his most important discovery. Returning from a holiday, he found his petri dishes of staphylococci bacteria cultures—part of an experiment he had been conducting—were all overgrown, except one. In this dish, there was only mold growing where there had once been bacteria.

A tidier and less observant person would have dumped out all these dishes, disappointed in a spoiled experiment. But Fleming took a closer look and slowly got excited about his discovery of a mold that could kill bacteria. He first nicknamed it mold juice and later called it penicillin. "When I woke up just after dawn on September 28, 1928, I certainly didn't plan to revolutionize all medicine by discovering the world's first antibiotic, or bacteria killer," he said. "But I suppose that was exactly what I did."

Fleming spent the next ten years trying to produce enough mold juice to keep up with his experiments, but he became discouraged when drug companies showed no interest in his work.

Howard Florey and Ernst Boris Chain, Fleming's colleagues from Oxford University, kept the promise of penicillin alive, proving it cured infections in mice. Penicillin became available to wounded soldiers halfway through World War II. This new miracle drug meant fewer soldiers lost limbs or died from infection. Sir Alexander Fleming, Sir Howard Florey, and Sir Ernst Boris Chain shared the Nobel Prize for medicine in 1945.

The Devastating Polio Epidemics

The warm weather came early in 1937, when a terrible polio epidemic hit Toronto, Canada. Several kids in our neighborhood disappeared into the Hospital for Sick Children and I can still feel the panic. Daily newspaper headlines cautioned parents to keep their children home, but my mother, Sadie Barnett, took that warning several steps farther. We were strictly forbidden to play with our friends and banned from answering the door, and hand-washing was frequent and thorough. My parents whispered late into the night, and we seven children had our ears to the wall.

One evening, Father announced we were leaving for the country—before school was out for the summer holidays—and we'd stay until after the first frost. Our excitement was squashed by his flash of anger as he reminded us we were more fortunate than others, having a safe place to go.

These were the late days of the Great Depression—before Canada had health care for everyone. Parents couldn't afford doctor bills, so they waited to see if their child really had polio before seeking medical attention. But the symptoms were vague and flu-like—queasy stomach, headache, sore muscles, and so on.

Not much was known about the disease then, but one thing was certain. In some cases, kids became paralyzed, their limbs withered. Or sometimes their throats seized up and they couldn't swallow or even breathe properly. We knew that you were most likely to get polio if you were young—like me and my siblings.

That summer at the cottage was like living in a parallel universe. Most days, I walked a quiet country road to the nearest village and bought a Toronto newspaper. I read that pools and parks had closed and that kids weren't allowed in theaters or even churches.

And the authorities were threatening to close down the Canadian National Exhibition on Children's Day—a rite of childhood at Toronto's annual fair. I went swimming in the lake every afternoon and enjoyed the outdoors with my brothers and sisters, glad that my parents had decided on our family quarantine.

There was no cure for polio, and the paper was full of debates among medical scientists. Some favored a liquid called convalescent serum (a serum obtained from a person who has recovered from the infection already, like a vaccine). Others believed that a nasal spray could prevent the virus from entering the body through the nose.

Eventually, both medicines proved useless. What did seem to help was a respirator called an iron lung. The Hospital for Sick Children had one such machine, and in August of that summer, it saved the life of a young girl whose lungs were paralyzed by polio.

When another child was admitted needing an iron lung, they built another "lung" using a respirator for premature babies and a wooden box. Nicknamed the lumber lung, it did the trick. The

results were so dramatic that more were made in the hospital basement.

Around that time, I developed a headache, fever, and a painful, stiff neck. I hid my symptoms from Mother because she'd "freak out," as my grandchildren would say now, and make me stay in bed. It was hot and I wanted to swim with my brother Victor, so I kept quiet and felt better in a few days.

It wasn't until I was in medical school five years later that I learned that most people who got sick during the epidemic didn't know they had the disease. They made complete recoveries. With the help of my medical school classmates, I found physical reminders of my bout with polio. I have one shriveled muscle in the back of my neck and a weak muscle in one upper arm. That's probably why I never made the baseball team in high school.

— Henry Barnett

To learn more about polio, the authors of this book interviewed their dad, Henry, about his personal experience with a polio epidemic. Now that he's ninety, Henry looks back and realizes he was very lucky—especially compared to his friend and classmate Hugh MacMillan, who, thirteen years later at the age of twenty-nine, was struck hard with polio.

Dr. Hugh MacMillan's wife was hospitalized with polio in 1950, and Hugh was a faithful visitor—until he too came down with the disease. She made a complete recovery, but he became paralyzed.

Unable to move from the neck down, Hugh required an iron lung machine. But gritty determination and extensive therapy brought back some movement and he eventually spent time out of the iron lung with the help of a special rocking chair and a technique—called frog breathing—of gulping down air.

With support from his family and friends, he invented devices that kept him independent and as productive as possible, including tools that enabled him to play cards, make phone calls, and feed himself. In the last few years of his life, he worked at the Ontario Crippled Children's Centre where he was a fantastic role model for disabled youngsters. Although he died in 1964, his example provides inspiration for many physically disabled people today.

President Franklin D. Roosevelt, a paralyzed polio victim since 1921, founded the National Foundation for Infantile Paralysis (NFIP) in 1938. From the beginning, the NFIP held an annual fundraising campaign nicknamed the March of Dimes after a song popular during the Great Depression called "Buddy, Can You Spare A Dime?" North Americans generously donated pocket change.

In 1947, the foundation hired Jonas Salk, an American medical doctor who specialized in virus research. Devoting his efforts to polio, Salk's work helped isolate the three kinds of polio in an effort to eventually develop a vaccine. Called the "summer plague," because the disease usually struck in the heat of the summer, polio continued to terrorize North America. The worst polio outbreak occurred in 1952, with fifty-eight thousand cases reported in the United States alone.

That same year, Salk's laboratory made a vaccine from killed polio virus. He tested it on children who already had polio before giving it to himself, his wife, his children, and volunteers. The vaccine, proven safe and effective, was then administered nationally to over a million kids—with amazing results.

In 1957, the March of Dimes sponsored a campaign to immunize all children in America, and the number of cases dropped to 5,600 that year and down to 121 by 1964. It became clear that polio could be beaten. Salk did not patent his discovery, hoping a low-cost vaccine would reach more people.

In 2011, WHO, UNICEF, Rotary International, and the Bill and Melinda Gates Foundation (Microsoft's founder) spearheaded the final push to rid the world of polio. Africa and India still have outbreaks, but Afghanistan and Pakistan are the only countries where new polio patients are regularly diagnosed.

India is using 2.3 million volunteer vaccinators to reach the most isolated and impoverished communities. Carrying the precious liquid in coolers and wearing bright yellow vests, volunteers approach mothers and their babies wherever they find them—in railway stations, markets, and on the street. Once a child is vaccinated, his or her fingernail is marked with permanent marker.

Meningitis

Dad found Tyler in his bedroom. He flicked on the light, asking, "How did the soccer tournament go?"

His son groaned and snarled, "Turn off the light. It hurts my eyes."

The room stank of vomit and the boy's forehead was scorching hot.

Dad peppered him with questions. "When did this start? Where does it hurt? Are any of your teammates sick?"

Tyler's voice was slurred as he murmured details of a headache and wanting to sleep.

Dad's worry turned to chilling fear when he focused on Tyler's foot, which was flung outside the bed sheets. The skin on his ankle and toes was purple, blotched, and swollen tight. Dad's brain screamed, "Call 911. This is a medical emergency!"

Tyler was losing consciousness by the time the ambulance arrived. Jake, the paramedic, called ahead to the ER and then slickly jabbed Tyler's thigh with an intramuscular injection of antibiotics. He started the IV as Tyler's pulse dipped dangerously low. Tyler was headed for septic shock.

With this strain of meningitis, minutes count and the ER team cranked into high gear. First the ABCs: airway clear, breathing shallow and rapid, circulation in distress. Start the IV fluids pronto and inject the first dose of steroids to reduce brain swelling. Give more antibiotics—try and beat the infection before it kills the skin and underlying tissues. Heart and blood pressure monitors …

In just a few hours, Tyler had transformed from a healthy eighteen-year-old into a critically ill patient in the intensive care unit. What he'd thought was the beginning of flu was actually meningococcal (bacterial) meningitis. It probably started when he borrowed a teammate's water bottle the day before.

He would spend two weeks in the hospital, lose parts of two toes on his left foot, and be scarred by raised and twisted markings on his ankle and leg. His recovery was slow and painful, but he considered himself lucky. He wasn't brain damaged—he could see and hear. And soccer was still his game.

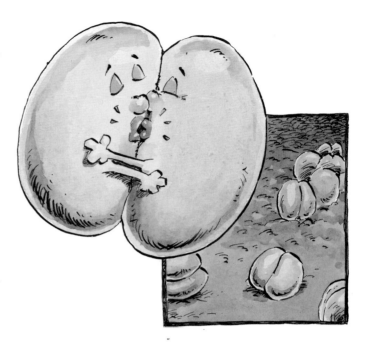

Anyone can get meningitis, but it's most likely to infect children under a year old in settings such as daycares and nursery schools, or young adults gathered together in army barracks, camping quarters, school cafeterias, and dorms. In Tyler's case, kids traveling as a team—sharing a bus in close quarters, grabbing a water bottle when thirsty—set the stage for an outbreak of meningitis.

It's a mystery why some people get sick while others don't. If someone does get sick, the best public health response is for family members and others in close contact to immediately take antibiotics. Vaccines prevent some

of the severest strains of meningitis, and some colleges and camps even require their visitors to be vaccinated before attending. If Tyler had it to do over …

Meningitis is caused by inflamed meninges—the sensitive membranes protecting the outside of the brain and spinal cord. Although sometimes caused by a fungus or traumatic brain injury, or as a complication from surgery, meningitis usually starts with an ordinary infection. The microbes travel through the bloodstream, ending up in the meninges. Meningitis takes hold and rapidly transforms into a different, much nastier illness.

Viral meningitis is the most common form of the disease. Usually, people fully recover without long-term side effects. Because it's a virus, antibiotics don't work. Instead, patients need rest, fluids, and painkillers for about ten days.

The bacterial form of meningitis is vicious but rare. It strikes hard and fast—sometimes killing its victim in a single day. Bacterial meningitis kills up to one in ten infected people. Untreated, it is fatal half the time.

Both types of meningitis start with the same symptoms: stiff neck, vomiting, fever, extreme crankiness, no energy, loss of appetite, and a headache that is sudden and sharp. Getting the right diagnosis and care at this point is critical. Doctors might start antibiotics before the test results are in, alarmed by the downward spiral of the sick patient. And the drugs can stop the savage destruction that bacterial meningitis inflicts on the body and even save life itself.

What do two kissing kidney beans have to do with meningitis? Medical students learn about hundreds of diseases and use tricks to remember them. Under the microscope, the bacterium that causes meningococcal meningitis looks like two kidney beans facing each other and sharing a kiss, their "bodies" forming a small doughnut shape. And you can get meningitis from kissing or from being in very close contact with someone who has the illness. Now you won't forget, either.

African Meningitis Belt

Like a perfect storm, meningitis has found the world's weak spot—it stretches from Ethiopia in the east to Senegal and Gambia in the west. This meningitis belt, as it is sometimes called, is a dusty, windswept African region that is in constant upheaval from war, famine, and poverty. It is home to the world's biggest concentration of meningitis outbreaks, epidemics, and deaths.

With the financial backing of the Gates Foundation, the Meningitis Vaccine Program aims to stamp out meningitis epidemics in Africa. In its first year (2010–11), twenty million people received injections of a vaccine developed with Gates's money. Each dose cost fifty cents.

AIDS: A Modern Plague

Curious children kibitz on the wharf as the boat's engine cuts and passengers hop ashore. This remote island on Lake Victoria, Tanzania, doesn't get many visitors, but these ones know the drill.

The children and a large group of other villagers escort the small contingent of international health workers to the chief's hut.

He's getting creaky with age and no longer walks down to meet outsiders. Hugging and clasping hands show respect and friendship, and sharing tea is a welcome activity on a dusty, hot day. Through an interpreter, they chat about weather, livestock, and the chief's grandson's wooden carvings—keeping things light.

Finally, the chief points out three of his people who need medical attention. One health worker produces the testing kits and demonstrates in mime how to swab one end along the soft tissue on the inside of the cheek until it's coated with saliva. The three testing swabs are laid out on a table and conversation resumes for an agonizing twenty minutes. A health worker examines the swabs one by one, and the results are clear on his smiling face. All three test negative for HIV.

Now the doctor can check for another cause for the local outbreak of diarrhea and weight loss— malnutrition, hookworm, yellow fever, or malaria—and hopefully help them heal. Nothing positive comes from being HIV positive.

In 1980, a new illness first known as the slim disease was reported around the Lake Victoria region of Eastern Africa, which includes Kenya, Uganda, and Tanzania. About the same time, otherwise healthy young men from the gay community in San Francisco and New York were seeking medical care for an alarming new disease. Researchers in the United States and France soon identified HIV—a unique and incurable disease.

The acronym HIV stands for human immunodeficiency virus. We can learn details about the disease by looking at the words that make up the acronym. It is a disease that is specific to humans (*H*), one that attacks the body's immune system (*I*), and it is a rapidly changing virus (*V*)—not a bacterium. The immune system is the very system designed to fight infectious illness, so once this disease takes hold, victims become more vulnerable to other illnesses.

AIDS, the second and terminal stage of HIV, stands for acquired immune deficiency syndrome. Again, look at the words in the acronym. The disease is not hereditary, meaning that it doesn't run in families. Rather, it is acquired (*A*). Immune deficiency (*I* and *D*) relate to how the disease strikes the cells and organs that keep the body well. Finally, AIDS is a classified as a syndrome (*S*) because it is a complex combination of symptoms, not a single disease.

Like many other serious illnesses, HIV starts out like the flu, lasting three or four weeks. Sometimes, those infected will experience a lull, or latent phase, of several months or as long as ten years. During this time, individuals are infectious, but many don't show symptoms even though their immune systems are slowly failing.

The immune system has several layers of defense. On the outside, skin acts as a protective barrier. Inside the body, in the bloodstream, phagocytes gorge on infectious microbes while infection-fighting chemicals are released when the immune system calls for help. The strongest and most specific defenders in the blood are the T cells and B cells, which are white cells produced in bone marrow.

When HIV gets in the body, it starts replicating itself by invading and killing white cells, specifically the

CD4+ T helper cells. When healthy, these helper cells check out all the other cells, making sure they are normal. When they discover abnormal cells, CD4+ T cells activate other cells designed to kill infections.

HIV gradually kills off so many helper cells that the body can't activate its own defenses. At this point, HIV is called AIDS, and the patient usually dies of a secondary infection such as tuberculosis, pneumonia, or one of several types of cancer such as Kaposi's sarcoma or non-Hodgkin's lymphoma.

Since 1981, researchers have scrambled for answers to three big questions: Where did HIV/AIDS come from? How is HIV spread? What are the symptoms and treatments?

Researchers found that a similar disease occurs in chimpanzees, other monkeys, domestic livestock, and lions. Most scientists accept the theory that hunters living in Cameroon, West Africa, were the first to contract this HIV-like illness from improperly cooked bush meat, such as chimpanzees. And it's believed that it took two hundred to four hundred years to morph into what we now call HIV, moving into Europe in 1939 with returning settlers. Several cases of HIV have been documented from the mid-1960s. The disease reached epidemic proportions in the 1980s.

Unlike some highly infectious viruses, HIV is not simple to catch. It doesn't spread through the air, water, or insect bites. HIV can't survive on household surfaces. In a health-care setting, spilled blood is cleaned up with a disinfectant as a precaution. HIV is spread from an infected or infectious person's blood and reproductive fluids—semen, breast milk, and vaginal secretions. If a healthy person comes in direct contact with infected reproductive fluids or blood by mouth, needle, or sexual activity, or through an open cut, HIV can develop.

By 1985, a blood test was invented to identify HIV-positive people. Since then, blood and organ donors are screened, eliminating these sources of infection. But HIV can still pass through the placenta of an infected mother into the bloodstream of a fetus.

By early 2010, 33.3 million people worldwide were HIV positive—that's about the same as the population of Canada. Twenty-five million died of AIDS between 1981 and 2011.

Symptoms of HIV include rapid weight loss, ongoing diarrhea, night sweats, swollen glands, memory loss, depression, and skin blotches. Without treatment, full-blown AIDS takes hold and death by infection or cancer will follow within about ten years.

Billions of dollars have been spent searching for an HIV/AIDS vaccine, but because the HIV virus changes very rapidly, there is no vaccine yet. Combinations of antiviral drugs, sometimes called cocktails, keep the virus from entering the AIDS phase and allow HIV patients to lead a "normal" life. The price tag is huge, so millions of HIV patients cannot afford treatment. Scientists are urgently searching for better, cheaper drugs and a vaccine, hoping to neutralize the virus before it changes and outsmarts the current treatment.

Without a cure or a vaccine, prevention is still the best solution. Education about the importance of clean needles and safe sex using condoms has lowered infection rates. But HIV remains a huge menace in Africa, home to 68 percent of all people living with the disease. The United Nations estimates that 14.8 million children in sub-Saharan Africa are orphans of parents who died of AIDS, living on their own or being raised by their grandparents, older siblings, or caregivers in orphanages.

AIDS has drastically changed the health of whole populations. In Botswana, for example, the average lifespan was over sixty years in the late 1960s but has now dropped to mid-forties. The disease kills the working segment of the population—mothers and fathers who put food on the table; who earn money for clothes, education, and health care; and who bind families together with love and caring. In the worst-hit parts of Africa, it is common for people to deny illness and to avoid testing because an HIV-positive test result translates into dying alone, cast out from family and community.

Although scientists predict we will see more new infections in the future—maybe worse than AIDS—there is some hope. Education and prevention programs, such as the Global Health Program, sponsored by the Bill and Melinda Gates Foundation, have increased the number of sub-Saharan Africans who get tested for HIV and receive free drugs. The goal is to stop the transmission of the virus and to enter a time when all communities test negatively—just as the three Africans did in the village on the shores of Lake Victoria, Tanzania, in 2004.

GLOBAL VILLAGE

Jumping Species

There's nothing new about diseases that hop, skip, or jump from one species to another. Living in close quarters with animals or making contact with their blood, feces, nasal secretions, or sputum has exposed us to cross-species, or zoonotic, infections for thousands of years.

Viruses rarely make the jump, but it's not hard for them to do so. All they need is a willing or vulnerable host. *Mycobacterium bovis*, a near relative of tuberculosis, started as an ailment specific to cows and spread to people through infected milk, emerging as TB over time. Now, TB moves from person to person without the cow connection.

HIV/AIDS is also an illness that crossed over from another species (chimpanzees) and established itself as a new and deadly human disease. These well-known cross-species infections didn't exactly jump—they crawled. It took both TB and HIV/AIDS many years to become established in the human population, requiring intimate contact for infection to occur. Still, their impacts now are worldwide and classified as pandemic.

Ever since the Spanish flu went global in 1918, public health and medical researchers have been on high alert, expecting the next big jump of a highly infectious disease, and predicting a catastrophic pandemic sometime in the future. A children's rhyme from the time of the Spanish flu describes both the speed and randomness of this fearsome virus:

I had a little bird.
And its name was Enza.
I opened the window,
And in-flew-Enza.

Children chanting these words could not have known that birds were the villains to watch for.

In 1996, a British woman contracted an avian flu virus (H7N7) from poop in a duck's crate. She developed an eye infection after a contaminated piece of straw flicked into her eye while she was cleaning. Luckily, she recovered, no one else got sick, and the infection stopped there.

Reports of a new avian influenza virus (H5N1, or bird flu) filtered out of China and Hong Kong one year later. The virus was ripping through domestic bird stocks. This virus was alarming—both violent and virulent, and very infectious. Up to 90 percent of infected poultry died—many developed internal bleeding and hemorrhaged to death within forty-eight hours.

In May 1997, a three-year-old boy from a Hong Kong farming community was diagnosed with—and died from—the bird flu. H5N1 had made the jump. The boy's death triggered a mass culling of 1.5 million domestic birds, effectively eliminating the outbreak in both people and birds.

In total, eighteen people had been infected by bird flu and six died. It wasn't exactly a pandemic, but the "if" factor stirred up fear.

If H5N1 had mutated and the virus had spread from person to person, authorities estimate that between 180 million and 360 million people would have died. These dire predictions

never came true, but the virus has not gone away. Rather, it has spread, turning up in more than fifteen countries in Southeast Asia and the Middle East. During the first half of 2011, the World Health Organization reported forty-eight cases of H5N1, with twenty-four deaths in Egypt, Cambodia, and Bangladesh, where avian influenza virus is active among domestic poultry.

Have you ever mucked out a pigpen? Forking straw and doing the chores, pig farmers are routinely exposed to swine influenza, but it doesn't usually jump the species barrier. When it does make the leap, sometimes farm workers or veterinarians have a mild case of swine flu and develop antibodies to the virus without ever knowing they've been exposed. Or they might come down with full-blown zoonotic swine flu and experience the usual symptoms: fever, sore throat and muscles, headache, and five days of feeling horrible.

In 2009, a new swine flu called H1N1 emerged, first appearing in Mexico and the southern United States. This was a flu cocktail of four different flu viruses—North American swine flu, human flu, Asian and European flu, and bird flu. H1N1 was nasty, lodging in people's lungs, causing respiratory distress and failure. And it was hitting and killing anyone—not just those usually vulnerable to flu.

The Director-General of WHO, Dr. Margaret Chan, issued a phase 6 warning to the global press on June 11, 2009. News headlines pushed the pandemic panic button: "Swine flu is back!" "Is there enough vaccine?" "Who gets vaccinated first?" "Pork sales drop as pandemic spreads."

The response to a pending pandemic was mixed. Some people refused to be vaccinated, worrying that it would make them sick. Others, such as American President Barack Obama,

WHO identifies six phases created to monitor and report influenza:

1. An influenza virus is active in animals but not humans
2. A small group of humans is infected with a zoonotic virus
3. The disease is mild and begins spreading human to human, but it is still localized
4. Larger scale outbreak occurs, and concern is rising about the threat of a possible pandemic
5. Virus is spreading among humans in more than one country
6. Outbreak has reached a global scale; the virus is on the move

set the example by rolling up his sleeve for a flu shot. Looking back, the fear was real and there were tragic deaths— young teens playing hockey or going to school one day were dead a few days later. When the flu fizzled out in August 2010, 18,138 people had died of H1N1 worldwide. The tally was higher than the usual flu season, but not as high as expected.

Today, doctors worry that people are "flu-ed out." In the fall of 2010, fewer people lined up for flu shots than normal. But what if …

SARS—Pandemic Panic

A surgical specialist paced outside the Hospital for Sick Children in Toronto, Canada. He watched the helicopter land on the rooftop, unload its precious cargo, and take off. The transplant suite was calling for the medical team, and he was locked outside, denied access to the hospital.

As a senior staff on weekend call, he had advance warning and biked to work, knowing the surgery would take all day. Peddling past gardens full of spring flowers, he had experienced the familiar bittersweet feeling. A child had died—and now another had a chance at life.

Locking up his bike, he realized he'd left his ID badge at home. SARS protocols were in place, and the hospital was on high alert. Everyone entered through the main door, showed current ID, used hand sanitizer, and was inspected by a security guard. There were no exceptions. His daughter better get here with his badge ASAP.

Meanwhile, Melanie and her husband were playing their own waiting game in Guelph—their first child was overdue. Their anxiety peaked when their midwife phoned with the news that the SARS outbreak had reached their community west of Toronto.

Melanie remembers, "Our midwife gave us the update: the Guelph General Hospital was in epidemic mode. Patients were triaged in tents set up in the parking lot, processed by gloved and masked nurses. Wait times could be long because everyone was thoroughly screened for SARS. If I was admitted, my husband would not be allowed into the hospital with me— maybe not even our midwife. After giving birth, I might be quarantined, and I'd be allowed only one visitor. The thought of being isolated in a hospital where people might have SARS terrified me. I could get it— so could our baby. That's when we decided on a home birth. With the midwife's care, our newborn daughter stayed safely at home until the SARS epidemic was over. That was the first time we'd ever considered that a hospital was a place where you could get sick as opposed to a place of healing. And that was very scary."

In southern China's Guangdong Province, the 2002 cold and flu season started as usual. November rains always led to more hospital admissions. Fever, chills, aches, and headaches were nothing new. A few days after being admitted, some patients developed rasping, dry coughs on top of their other symptoms.

This looked like severe pneumonia, but antibiotics did nothing. Was it a virus? Antivirals didn't work either. Patients got sicker and needed ventilators to catch their breath. And one in ten patients were dying—a higher rate than usual for pneumonia. Doctors were puzzled. It wasn't long before the health workers and undertakers started getting sick, too.

Guangdong Province had never seen a disease like this before. The Chinese government kept the lid on the outbreak, issuing neither official news reports nor health alerts. But frightened families took their sick beyond the outbreak area, hoping for better medical attention. Traveling by train, these patients infected fellow passengers and spread the disease to the provincial capital.

When Dr. Liu Jianlun, a doctor who had worked long hours at a hospital in Guangdong, traveled by bus to Hong Kong for a wedding on February 21, 2003, he was incubating the illness. The elevator and the ninth floor of his hotel became the launching pad for a global pandemic.

On February 23, an American businessman named Johnny Chen left his ninth-floor hotel room and checked out. He flew to Hanoi, Vietnam, and was admitted to hospital six days later with pneumonia-like symptoms. Concerned it might be the mystery illness from China, the Hanoi hospital notified the World Health Organization.

Dr. Carlo Urbani, an infectious disease specialist working for WHO in Hanoi, was assigned the case. He identified the new disease and called it SARS—severe acute respiratory syndrome—giving it an acronym with four fearsome words. A few weeks later, both he and his patient, Johnny Chen, were dead from the disease, but his timely work is credited with grabbing public attention and helping stop the outbreak.

Before it had a name, SARS flew into Canada with a seventy-eight-year-old woman named Kwan Sui-chu, who had ridden the hotel elevator in Hong Kong on February 21, 2003, with Dr. Liu. She died of a supposed heart attack on March 5, soon after returning home. WHO issued a global alert for SARS on March 12. When Kwan's forty-four-year-old son died of pneumonia on March 13, the authorities suspected SARS had checked into Toronto.

As soon as SARS spread beyond China's borders, the disease became headline news for five months. Questions swirled. What was this new deadly disease and how did it start? Was this epidemic headed in the direction of the Spanish flu pandemic?

Could anyone predict where it would turn up next?

Medical response teams raced to identify and trace all cases of infection, isolating and quarantining any patients. China, suddenly under scrutiny, lifted the veil of secrecy and urged citizens to wear masks, wash hands, and report any sick people to the authorities.

Widespread fear and real danger of infection kick-started the international health community into action, and global war was declared on SARS. Reports of illness were circulated daily, a process organized by WHO's head office in Geneva, Switzerland, the Center for Disease Control and Prevention in Atlanta, and "war rooms" in SARS hotspots around the world. These bulletins distributed all relevant information— new documented cases, laboratory findings, death tallies, travel advisories, respirator shortages, mask supplies, and isolation methods.

Within a few weeks, scientists knew that SARS is a coronavirus—the same culprit that causes the common cold. Detective work zeroed in on markets in Guangdong where wild animals were sold for their meat—workers handling the animals had been the first to fall sick with SARS. Civet cats—weasel-like animals—carry the coronavirus, and scientists believe they passed a variation of the virus on to their handlers.

Health workers were sure the infection spread through nasal droplets, but other research showed it was also a super-spreading virus—one individual carrier, showing no signs of illness, could infect many people. Tests also showed that the virus could live outside a human host for over twenty-four hours, making doorknobs, handles, counters—any surface where a sick person's sneeze could land—capable of passing on the virus.

This virulent virus required extreme, expensive measures to stop. Air travel to and from China was grounded, and international airports installed scanners to detect if travelers were feverish. Restaurants, theaters, conference centers, hotels, sports complexes, funeral homes, and places of worship were empty anywhere the SARS disease had been active.

Anyone who had been in contact with someone who had SARS was sent home from work for a self-monitored quarantine. In China, electronic ankle bracelets raised the alarm if quarantined persons left their homes. Lawbreakers faced stiff fines. In Canada alone, the travel industry lost over a billion dollars the spring SARS came to town.

SARS was the first pandemic that the world experienced immediately and collectively. The media hounded and hunted for information, raising awareness as well as panic. Rapid response, effective public health enforcement, and luck stopped SARS in its tracks—but not until it had spread through 31 countries, infecting 8,422 people, and killing 916.

Biological Warfare: Then and Now

The faces around the war room are somber. Some people cast their eyes down and shake their heads, digesting the command from their supreme leader. All other tactics have failed— too many of their soldiers are casualties in this crazy war. Their leader has decided to deploy biological weapons, deliberately inflicting a deadly illness on their enemy. Unfortunately, they can't protect innocent bystanders. Collateral damage is a consequence of biological war.

Can you imagine making this choice? Of course not! But in the past, tyrants, conquistadors, and unscrupulous military commanders have used biological weapons to their own advantage—even turning them on their own people. An international treaty signed at the Biological Weapons Convention in 1972 made it illegal to develop, produce, and use such weapons. But there is still a loophole—it's not illegal to make weapons to defend against a biological attack.

People at war have always looked for an added advantage. Biological weapons have been around for thousands of years, long before computer guided missiles. In 400 BC, without knowing how or why it worked, Scythian archers dipped arrow tips in poison—a festering mixture of blood, feces, and snake venom. Their wounded enemies died from toxic reactions or severe infections.

Hannibal, the Carthaginian commander, fought a famous naval battle in 184 BC against King Eumenes II, ruler of the ancient Greek city of Pergamon, using an unusual biological weapon—clay pots filled with poisonous snakes. Hannibal's soldiers hurled and smashed the pots onto the decks of the enemy's ships, sending King Eumenes's soldiers into a state of crazed confusion. They

lost the battle, leaving no record of the fate of the snakes.

Frederick Barbarossa, a twelfth century German Holy Roman Emperor, won a devastating victory over the people of Tortona, Italy. He poisoned their wells with the bodies of decomposing soldiers before reducing their town to rubble. Barbaric!

Bubonic plague victims were used as weapons of war from about 1346, when the Mongols catapulted plague corpses into the city of Caffa, Italy, until 1710, when Russians fighting Swedish forces catapulted infected dead bodies into the city of Reval (now Tallinn, Estonia), spreading panic. Plague likely came with fleas on the rats that scavenged these disgusting scenes.

And smallpox hit parts of North America disguised as gifts of blankets from explorers and soldiers, targeting the Native American peoples who had no immunities to this disease.

Thanks to microbiologists such as Koch and Pasteur, it is possible to isolate and store large quantities of specific bacteria and viruses. Researchers need these supplies for experiments and to develop vaccines—all for the general good. But in the wrong hands or used carelessly, these specimens can become weapons of mass destruction.

For example, research on the bacterium anthrax proved unpredictable and hard to control. Gruinard Island, off the northwest coast of Scotland, was the site of experiments using biological weapons during World War II. The island became so polluted with anthrax that it was off limits for forty years. After four years of cleanup using formaldehyde, the Department of Defense claimed the island was no longer contaminated with anthrax. A flock of sheep was introduced in 1990 but scientists and archaeologists fear some dormant anthrax spores remain and advise against traveling to the island.

In 1979, about a hundred people fell sick with a suspicious illness near the city of Sverdlovsk, Russia. When sixty-four died, the Soviet government issued an announcement that blamed meat contaminated with anthrax spores—an agricultural mishap. Soon after the Cold War ended, in 1992, President Boris Yeltsin admitted that anthrax spores accidentally leaked into the air from a secret weapons facility.

More recently, in Washington D.C., Bocca Raton, Florida, and New York City, terrorists were blamed for mailing anthrax spores to several media outlets and two United States Senators' offices. Five people died and seventeen were infected. This incident occurred in the month following the 9/11 attacks, sending an already jittery nation closer to the edge. What if terrorists dropped anthrax from a plane or blew it into the subway system?

A bomb of anthrax, or another lethal bacterium, has the potential of causing mass murder, but it has never happened. United Nations inspectors monitor suspicious facilities that could be manufacturing biological weapons, trying to keep the world safe from this kind of threat.

Are Your Vaccinations Up-To-Date?

Picture this scenario: It's your usual morning commute to school. You're sitting at the back of the near-full bus, watching the other passengers. Twins sitting near the front sneeze in unison. One complains loudly to the other, "Sneeze in your sleeve! You've already given me your flu. Think of others!" At the next stop, a mother gets on the bus carrying her small son, his sweaty head slumped on her shoulder. The swollen lymph glands on his neck are clearly visible. He's got mumps.

An elderly gentleman struggles up the stairs behind the mother. He's using two arm-braced canes. Post-polio syndrome grips his lower limbs, taking another round out of him seventy-five years after he survived a mild case in his youth. At the next stop, a teen flops down on the seat next to you, her face flushed and eyes blurry. She rubs the back of her neck and grimaces with an obvious headache. Diagnosis—meningitis.

A few stops later, on gets a young man with oozing, angry, red sores covering his face. He's visibly sweating despite the cold winter temperature. Could he have smallpox? What could be worse?

The next time the door opens, a dog bounds in with foam spewing from his mouth, his eyes wild, and fangs bared. Rabies!

Go back to the beginning of this page and reshoot the scene with a different cast of characters—fully vaccinated people and dog. This time, the ride will be a healthy one, although it could be boring.

You can still get flu from a fellow

The Making of a Seasonal Flu Shot

One needle jab and maybe a booster shot—and you are good for life. That's true of many childhood vaccinations. But the seasonal flu shot is different—for now.

Scientists study each year's influenza cases and carefully record their findings. One hundred and one countries share their data on the type and infectious qualities of the current strain of flu. Early in the year, this information is used to develop the upcoming flu season's vaccination. Scientists choose the viruses they think are most likely to cause infection the following flu season. Each seasonal influenza vaccine is a mixture of three influenza viruses: one each of influenza A and B virus, and one seasonal influenza virus.

Making a vaccine is a combination of hard fact, best guess, and luck. Once the elements of the vaccine are chosen, flu vaccine factories have about six months to crank out millions of doses. Fertilized chicken eggs are injected with the virus, kept warm and incubated for a few days, and then live virus is harvested from the eggs. The live virus is killed and packaged in vials, which nurses and doctors later draw from with needles. Researchers continue to look for a one-shot cure for flu. Until then, WHO recommends that young and old people, as well as front-line health workers, get their shot every year. Does that include you?

bus traveler—there is no perfect vaccine for flu. And the older man with post-polio symptoms will struggle up the stairs, but he can't infect you with polio. This is life as you've come to expect it. Many diseases no longer threaten populations because of routine vaccinations.

But there are people who believe that vaccinations are sometimes harmful and should be optional. A recent example occurred in Britain in response to a 1998 article published in the respected medical journal *The Lancet*. Dr. Andrew Wakefield's research mistakenly connected the measles vaccine with autism (a developmental disorder). Some concerned parents decided against giving their children the MMR vaccine. The number of measles and mumps cases increased sharply—some resulting in death and others leading to serious medical complications.

If no one is vaccinated against a disease, everyone is at risk—as was the case with SARS. When 100 percent are immune, a disease becomes extinct, which is what happened with smallpox. Although the ideal public health scenario would be for all people to be vaccinated, it's not essential—as long as enough are immune. In this case, the population is protected by herd immunity—the percentage of people who could get sick is low enough that an epidemic outbreak is impossible. The threshold for herd immunity—the percentage needed to prevent an outbreak—varies from one disease to another, depending on the virulence of the disease and how easily it spreads.

If you asked a group of seven-year-olds whether needles should be optional, they'd almost surely answer yes. But there are serious consequences if you choose not to be vaccinated. Is such a choice equivalent to smoking or to drinking and driving? Join in the debate—what is your view on personal choice and rights when it comes to health?

Big Lessons from Pandemics

After reading this book, are you surprised you are alive? Your ancestors lived long enough to become parents. But after that, they may have suffered and died from an infectious disease such as bubonic plague, tuberculosis, malaria, measles, or Spanish flu.

Run the gauntlet of pandemic outbreaks over the past five thousand years and three big lessons stand out. These lessons may seem like common sense to you, but they took ages to learn. And although your ancestral

of a private detective, the New York City Health Department, and police to figure out where the outbreak started. The common thread turned out to be a recent immigrant from Ireland who worked as a domestic servant in seven different homes. Mary Mallon cooked meals and took trays to sick family of her employers, including a little girl who died. How could Mary be the culprit? She was perfectly healthy.

Typhoid, or enteric fever, is transmitted through salmonella bacteria found in feces and urine. A person can catch typhoid by drinking water or eating food that has been handled by an infectious person who hasn't washed properly. Mary Mallon never showed typhoid symptoms of fever, diarrhea, or rash. Despite her protests, she was declared a "healthy carrier"—but not before she'd infected over fifty people, killing three of them. Nicknamed Typhoid Mary, she was quarantined for three years at a clinic on a nearby island, but she was later released after she promised to work in a laundry, not a kitchen.

Typhoid Mary did not keep her word but changed her name and took another cooking job. When typhoid flared up again in the city, she was tracked down and sent back to the island for the rest of her life.

pandemic survivors lived on, they suffered the painful loss of family, friends, and much more.

Lesson 1: Not all diseases disappear when the symptoms are gone and not all patients are honest about their health. The story of Mary Mallon:

Hospitals were built for the sick, but what about preventing illness? New York City faced this challenge between 1900 and 1907 when typhoid fever moved in. It took the combined efforts

The authorities can't banish healthy disease carriers to a lonely island any more, but they can enforce quarantine until the carriers are no longer a threat. Today, when somebody deliberately or willingly passes on an infectious disease, such as a fatal illness like AIDS, the authorities can imprison the person who spread the disease.

Lesson 2: Diseases have no sense of timing and can show up when people are already suffering and vulnerable. The story of famine, typhus, and immigration:

Lousy. Look up this word in your dictionary. You've never felt that bad! Rooted in the Middle Ages, lousy meant infested with lice. Now it's used as slang to describe feeling unwell.

An Irish immigrant in the 1840s had a different take on lousy. Evicted from his farm during the potato famine and desperate with hunger, his only chance was a new life in North America. He survived the trans-Atlantic voyage on a "coffin ship," but the horror would haunt him forever.

Travelers were crammed into the ship's hold without sufficient water or food. Endemic typhus broke out, a bacterial infection spread by bites from lice or contact with lice feces. Victims suffered high fevers, extreme headache, rash, chills, body aches, delirium, diarrhea, and vomiting all endured in cramped, disgusting conditions, over rough seas.

Records are incomplete, but at least one in six passengers died and was buried at sea. When the survivors reached North American ports, they were not welcomed by the locals. Scrawny and destitute, the immigrants brought lice and typhus ashore.

Typhus is now preventable by vaccine and treatable with antibiotics, but epidemics occur where crowded conditions break down hygiene, such as after a natural disaster or within refugee camps, or jails. Diseases such as typhus school us in cleanliness and prevention. Bathing ourselves, laundering our clothes and bedding, keeping a clean house, and—above all—hand-washing are practices that prevent many infections.

Lesson 3: The public health measures we take for granted can break down, so we have to stay on guard. The story of disease and death from contaminated water in a first world country:

"What took them so long?" is a theme of medical history. In the past, health workers, military commanders, and the general public repeatedly clung to old ideas because of ignorance, pride, or stubbornness. Luckily, curious scientists with careful observation skills kept trying.

Public health officers carry this lesson forward. Constantly working in the background, they tally new cases, check inventories of medications such as antivirals, and step forward when an infectious outbreak occurs. Health office bulletins remind us of the importance of routine vaccinations and recommend extra shots when flus such as H1N1 threaten our communities. We are better informed and prepared than our ancestors.

But even in wealthy countries, public health can break down on a basic level. When you turn on the tap at your home, what comes out? Clean, safe drinking water—right? That's what most readers of this book will assume. If you can detect a whiff of chemicals, like the smell of a swimming pool, you're living where water is monitored, treated with chlorine, and tested, and where waterlines are flushed and kept clean. That's what our municipal taxes help pay for!

If you heard that half the people in a small town suddenly became ill with bloody diarrhea, vomiting, and stomach cramps, you might think a pandemic illness had struck in a far off country. Actually, there was indeed a calamitous breakdown of water purification in May 2000 in the prosperous farming community of Walkerton, Canada.

An inquiry later reported that a series of preventable lapses added up to disaster: government cost cutting, inadequate monitoring, untrained staff, uncontrolled runoff from nearby cattle farms, and the failure of officials to investigate complaints of the smell of chlorine in the water. No one connected the dots before the tragedy, but the experience of Walkerton has changed how water is managed and delivered. And like many health-related lessons, we have learned that nothing can be left to chance.

Remembering the stories of Mary Mallon, potato famine refugees, and the people of Walkerton will help you survive. Along with what you've learned in this book about the past, you'll need good luck and keen observation. Your health is like a suit of armor, protecting your body with each link. Check to make sure your links are all strong. Vaccinations—check! Healthy food—check! Clean water—check! Wash your hands, sneeze into your sleeve, stay home and take your medicine when you're sick—check!

GLOSSARY

allergy: an unusually high sensitivity to a situation or substance, such as a food, pollen, or disease microorganism. Common symptoms of allergies include sneezing, itchiness, and skin rash.

ancestor: a relative, usually more remote than a grandparent, from whom a person is directly descended

antibiotic: a chemical substance produced by various molds and microorganisms that kills or weakens bacteria and some other microorganisms. Penicillin and streptomycin are examples of antibiotics that are used as medicines.

bacterium: a microscopic, single-celled organism that lives in colonies on or in the soil, water, or other organisms, including people; some species of bacterium cause disease. One bacterium; two or more bacteria.

cell: the smallest structural and functional unit of living organisms. Some cells can live as independent units, while others form colonies and are building blocks of more complicated organisms, such as plants and animals.

communicable disease: an infectious disease that can pass from an infected individual by direct or indirect contact to an unaffected individual through bodily fluids or by contact with an animal or insect carrier

contagion: the transmission or spreading of a disease by close contact

contagious disease: an infectious disease easily passed on to unaffected people by direct or indirect contact with infected individuals, their bodily fluids, or objects in the environment that they have contaminated

endemic: a word used to describe a contagious disease or condition that is present in a limited area and infecting a relatively small number of people

epidemic: the outbreak of a contagious disease, spreading from person to person, rapidly and widely, in an area where the disease is not otherwise common

immunity: the ability to resist a particular toxin or disease. People can be born with natural immunity to a disease, can develop immunity to future infection by surviving a bout of the disease, or can build up immunity by vaccination against the disease.

infection: an invasion of the body by a bacterium, virus, protozoan, or other disease-causing agent—and the body's reaction to it

infectious disease: a disease caused by the invasion of a microorganism, such as a fungus, bacterium, or virus, that enters an organism. Infectious diseases spread from person to person or from the environment to a person.

inoculation: the introduction of a substance to the body to increase immunity to a disease

miasma: an unhealthy or unpleasant smell or vapor, such as a smell rising from a swamp or decaying matter. It was once believed that miasma was poisonous.

microbe: a microscopic organism, especially a disease-causing bacterium, virus, or protozoan. Microbes are best seen under a microscope.

microscopic: a word used to describe something that is too small to be seen by the unaided eye but is big enough to be seen with the help of a microscope

organism: a form of life, such as a plant, animal, bacterium, protozoan, mold, or virus, that is composed of interdependent parts that maintain various vital processes

pandemic: an epidemic that spreads across a wide area, covering countries, continents, and even the whole world

parasite: an organism that lives on or in another organism of a different species and that gets its nutrition from the other organism's body

pathogen: a bacterium, virus, protozoan, or other microbe that causes disease—also called a germ *pestilence:* a usually fatal epidemic disease, such as bubonic plague

plague: a highly infectious, often fatal, epidemic disease. This term is sometimes used to refer to the bubonic plague.

pox: a disease, such as smallpox, that is characterized by skin eruptions. Sometimes the diseases smallpox and syphilis were nicknamed "the pox."

protozoan: a one-celled organism, usually microscopic, that has the ability to move in simple ways and/or carry disease

pustule: a small, inflamed raised eruption or rash on the skin that is filled with pus

resistance: the natural ability of an organism, such as a human being, to fight off or resist a microbe or poison. Also, the ability of disease microbes to withstand or resist the effects of a drug that once was lethal to the microbes.

symbiotic: a close, long-term association between two or more living organisms of different species that is usually mutually beneficial

vaccination: inoculation with a harmless form of a disease to stimulate immunity against that disease. Vaccinations may be given by needle, inhalation, or mouth.

vector: a carrier or transporter of disease, often an insect or mite. The rat flea is the vector whose bite carries bubonic plague from rats to people.

virus: an ultramicroscopic infectious agent. Viruses are not usually considered life forms because they will only grow and reproduce within the cells of a living host.

INDEX